HOLOCAUST

WRITTEN BY
ANGELA GLUCK WOOD

To Ryan
for memory and hope

Consultant Professor Dan Stone
Senior editors Francesca Baines, Claire Nottage
Senior art editors Owen Peyton Jones, Sarah Ponder
Editors Jenny Finch, Fran Jones, Andrea Mills,
Zahavit Shalev, Clare Zinkin
Art editor Marilou Prokopiou
Designers Jim Green, Spencer Holbrook,
Samantha Richiardi, Smiljka Surla, Jacqui Swan, Nihal Yesil
Managing editor Linda Esposito
Managing art editor Diane Thistlethwaite
Publishing manager Andrew Macintyre
Category publisher Laura Buller
Picture researchers Julia Harris-Voss, Kate Lockley,
Jo Walton, Debra Weatherley
Cartographer Ed Merritt
DTP designers Siu Chan, Andy Hilliard
Jacket editor Mariza O'Keeffe
Jacket design manager Sophia Tampakopoulos-Turner
Production controller Angela Graef
DVD project manager Anthony Pearson

This American paperback edition published 2008
First American Edition 2007
Published in the United States by DK Publishing, Inc.,
345 Hudson Street, New York, NY 10014

10 9 8 7 6

011-HD088-12/2007

Quotes taken from testimonies from the USC Shoah Foundation
Institute for Visual History and Education

A Cataloging-in-Publication record for this book
is available from the Library of Congress.

ISBN: 978-0-7566-3858-0

Color reproduction by Colourscan, Singapore
Printed and bound in Hong Kong

Discover more at www.dk.com

HOLOCAUST

the events and their impact on real people

WRITTEN BY
ANGELA GLUCK WOOD

CLINGING TO LIFE

THE END OF THE WAR

THE AFTERMATH

CONTENTS

The mission of the USC Shoah Foundation Institute for Visual History and Education is to overcome prejudice, intolerance, and bigotry—and the suffering they cause—through the educational use of the Institute's visual history testimonies. With nearly 52,000 video testimonies of Holocaust survivors and other witnesses, collected in 32 languages and from 56 countries, one of the Institute's primary goals is to provide the broadest possible access to these testimonies to people around the world. Throughout the pages of this book, and on the accompanying DVD, you will find first-person accounts of Holocaust survivors and other witnesses taken from the Institute's archive.

This symbol appears throughout the book after some of the quotations of the survivors and witnesses, indicating that the DVD contains testimony clips from that particular person.

THE BOOK YOU ARE HOLDING *in your hands is unique. While it is an authoritative history of the Holocaust that combines text and images in an altogether uncommon way, it is also a human record of the Shoah and its meaning. The pages that follow are replete with statistics and facts, many of them nothing short of horrifying. But these pages also contain the faces and the words of men and women who survived the murderous anti-Semitic world of Nazi-dominated Europe.*

You will also find another singular feature packaged along with this volume, a DVD containing video interviews of many of the survivors whose names are contained in these pages. These men and women spoke of their experiences directly and candidly to the cameras and microphones of the USC Shoah Foundation Institute for Visual History and Education.

The work of the Institute—which was originally called Survivors of the Shoah Visual History Foundation—is the most important professional work of my life. I am deeply proud of its accomplishments and truly thrilled that you will have the opportunity to learn about the Holocaust through the group of testimonies assembled for this book and the accompanying DVD.

Steven Spielberg

FOREWORD
BY STEVEN SPIELBERG

THE JEWS OF EUROPE

FOR MORE THAN 2,000 YEARS Jews have
lived in small communities in societies
throughout Europe, but it was only from
the late 18th century that they were able
to play a bigger role in society. The center
of the Jewish community has always been
the synagogue, and even nonpracticing
Jews still feel very much part of the Jewish
community and its story.

The Passover ceremony
Jewish family life has always been important. Each spring,
families celebrate together the festival of Passover to remember
the time when their ancestors were slaves in Egypt, but God
set them free. This 15th-century illustration shows the special
Passover meal (Seder) during which Jews tell stories, sing songs,
and remember and retell the experience of escaping slavery.

Beginning of the Golden Age
of Spain, with freedom of
religion under Muslim rule

The printing press is
invented in Germany
by Johannes Gutenberg

After the Romans destroy the
Temple in Jerusalem, Jews are
forced to leave Judea to live in
communities throughout Europe
and the world

Christianity
becomes the official
religion of the
Roman Empire

North African
Muslims conquer
Spain

Between 1347 and 1353 the
"Black Death" (bubonic plague)
kills a third of the population
of Europe

EUROPE

| c. 33 | 70 | 100 | c. 400 | 622 | c. 700 | c. 900 | 1099 | 1271 | 1347 | 1450 | 1453 |

WORLD

The beginning
of the Christian
Church

Buddhism spreads
to China from the
Indian subcontinent

Rise of Islam,
spreading from the
Arabian Peninsula

Christian Crusaders capture
Jerusalem and kill thousands
of Muslims and Jews

Constantinople (now Istanbul),
the capital of the Eastern Roman
Empire, falls to the Turks

The Italian
explorerer Marco
Polo reaches China

The beginnings of the Protestant Reformation of the Catholic Church

The Unification of Germany—the northern and southern states join to form a German Empire

First Zionist Congress held in Switzerland

In a royal edict, Jews and Muslims are expelled from Spain

The French Revolution sees the end of the rule of the monarchy in France

The map of Europe is redrawn at the Congress of Vienna

The Dreyfus Affair exposes anti-Semitism in France

Adolf Hitler becomes chancellor of Germany

1492   1517   1518   1620   1789   1791   1815   1871   1894   1897   1914   1917   1933   1939

Europeans transport the first African slaves to the West Indies

Russian Jews are forced to live in a restricted area, known as a "Pale of Settlement"

World War I begins (to 1918)

World War II begins (to 1945)

Italian sailor Christopher Columbus leads a Spanish expedition and reaches the land mass later named "America"

English religious dissenters set sail in the Mayflower for Virginia in America

The Russian Revolution sees the czar abdicate and the Bolsheviks (communists) take over

9

THE ORIGINS OF THE JEWS

ALTHOUGH THE ORIGINS OF THE JEWS lie in the Middle East, today there are Jewish communities in many countries, with the largest numbers in Israel, North America, and Europe. Over the centuries, Jews in Europe were driven out of the lands they had settled and forced to find another home. This led to the description the "wandering Jew."

In the Land of Israel
The Jewish people began as slaves in Egypt, about 3,000 years ago until, they believe, God freed them and promised them their own land, which they called Israel. In their capital, Jerusalem, they built the Temple, as a center for worship and charitable work. In Jerusalem today there is a large walk-around model of the ancient city, showing the beauty of the Temple.

Deportation to Babylonia
About 2,500 years ago the Babylonians invaded Jerusalem, destroyed the Temple, and carried off the educated and skilled Jews. Centuries later, when Babylonia had become Persia, Jews were once again under threat. But the Persian king, Ahasuerus, was married to Esther, a Jewish woman. As this image shows, she pleaded with him to save Jewish lives.

Exile under Roman rule
When the Jews returned from exile, they rebuilt Jerusalem and the Temple, but had to counter many invasions. About 2,000 years ago, the Romans occupied the land. The Jews were overpowered and in 70 CE the second Temple and much of Jerusalem was destroyed. This marble arch in Rome shows Jews being forced to carry the candelabrum that the Romans stole from the Temple.

Jewish movement in Europe

→ Expulsions
→ Dispersal
→ Migrations

Dates within orange boxes mark the major expulsions of Jews from Great Britain, France, and Spain.

ATLANTIC OCEAN

1290

1100

1492

Ashkenazi

1394

1350

1450

500–800

1492

Sephardic

Rome

Black Sea

Byzantium

Athens

Babylon

1492

Mediterranean Sea

Jerusalem

Alexandria

0 km 500 1,000 1,500
0 miles 500 1,000

The spread of Jews in Europe

When Jerusalem fell to the Romans in 70 CE, some Jews fled toward Babylonia to join the Jewish community there. Others joined communities in northern Africa and then Spain. Most were deported to Rome or settled elsewhere in Europe, as refugees. This map shows the main movements of Jews from that time to the present.

The Rhine and the Rhone

Jewish settlement in Europe was mostly beside rivers—for travel and trade. Communities around the Rhine (Germany) and the Rhone (France) became centers of Jewish culture. This German woodcut shows the lighting of a special lamp for the winter festival of Hanukkah.

An invitation and a charter

In 1264, the charter of King Boleslav of Poland granted Jews protection and they were invited to settle as administrators in the area that is now Lithuania, Belarus, and Ukraine. The Wistula River (above) on which they traveled became a symbol of their journeys to and from Poland.

The life of Jews in Spain

Sephardic Jews—those in Spain—enjoyed a Golden Age during Islamic rule. Although never treated as equal to Muslims, they were free to practice Judaism and Jewish culture flourished. Later, under Christian rule, however, most were forced to convert to Christianity or be killed—the rest were expelled in 1492. One family took with them this delicate handpainted Passover book.

A warm welcome

In 1492, news reached the Ottoman (Turkish) Empire that Jews were banished from Spain. Sultan Beyazit II, shown here, granted Jews safe haven in his empire and personally greeted them at the port. Most Jews settled and flourished in the European parts of the empire. Many of the sultans' doctors were Jewish, and it was Jews who set up the first printing presses.

THE JEWS OF SEFARAD

THE HEBREW WORD FOR SPAIN IS *Sefarad* and Sephardic Jews are those who originated in Spain or Portugal. When under Islamic rule, there were good relations between Jews and Muslims, but under Catholic rule, there was great pressure for Jews to convert. In 1492, both Jews and Muslims were expelled from Spain, and Jews fled to Muslim countries and the Netherlands.

Maimonides
The Jewish scholar Rabbi Moshe ben Maimon is better known as Maimonides. He was born in the 12th century in Cordoba, Spain, where this statue stands. He developed good relations with Muslim scholars and leaders and was highly respected as a doctor, philosopher, linguist, and specialist in Jewish law.

A secret life
Gracia Mendes was a wealthy Jewish widow living in Portugal during Christian rule. She stayed behind and lived a secret Jewish life while using her money and contacts to help Jews, forced to convert to Christianity under pain of death, to escape. She was hailed as a heroine. This modern image of her is by an American artist.

The Ladino language
When Spanish and Portuguese Jews settled in lands such as Turkey and the Balkans, they continued to speak the same language. This Latin-based language was called "Ladino'" and it became the unifying language of Sephardic Jews in Europe. Most Ladino-speaking Jews were murdered in the Holocaust and today very few speak the language. However, there is still interest in Ladino poetry and song.

A broad education
Sephardic Jews value traditional study, and wherever Jews were barred from schools, the Jewish community set up its own. In the late 19th century, the *Alliance Israélite Universelle*, a Jewish organization based in Paris, developed modern schools in several places, including Morocco (above). These schools combined religious education, secular learning, and practical skills.

Sephardic synagogues

In Muslim societies, synagogues resembled the style of mosques in many ways and often used the geometric shapes and swirling patterns of Islamic art. In Christian societies, synagogue art and architecture was more likely to resemble that of churches. This Sephardic synagogue in Florence in Italy, built in 1892, has some of the features of churches of the period as well as the domes and decoration found in mosques.

An estimated 250,000 Jews were expelled from Spain. They were not allowed to take money or valuables.

Sephardic weddings

Many Sephardic Jews, particularly in North Africa, begin wedding celebrations several days before the actual ceremony, with separate parties for the bride and the groom. Here, the female friends and relatives of a Sephardic bride sing and dance in her honor. Parties for the married couple are also held in the week after the wedding.

Ashkenazi Jews in Prague

From the 11th century, many Ashkenazi Jews settled in Prague, capital of the Czech Republic. The city became famous for its traditions of Jewish learning and hospitality, and became known as "A City and a Mother in Israel"—Israel meaning here the Jewish extended family. As this 19th-century painting shows, the clock on the Jewish town hall in Prague has Hebrew letters for the hours and runs counterclockwise, as Hebrew is read from right to left. The building on the left is the Altneu Shul, Europe's oldest functioning synagogue.

THE JEWS OF ASHKENAZ

ASHKENAZ IS THE OLD HEBREW word for Germany. When the Jews were expelled from Germany in the Middle Ages, those that settled in northern, central, and eastern Europe became known as "Ashkenazi." The language of Ashkenazi communities was Yiddish. This was based on medieval German, with some Hebrew expressions, as well as words from the languages of those places where the Jews settled.

The Golem of Prague

In the 16th-century, a series of disasters threatened the Jewish community of Prague. Ashkenazi folklore tells how Rabbi Loew created a manlike creature from clay—known by the Yiddish word golem—who had the power to save them. This legend formed the basis for the 1920 German film, *The Golem* (above).

Rashi of Troyes

The most highly respected Ashkenazi commentator was Rabbi Shlomo Yitzhak, known as Rashi, who lived in Troyes in France during the 11th century. His commentaries on the Bible were influential in his time and continue to be so today. In this monument in Troyes, the Hebrew letters for "Rashi" are carved out and a bright light shines through them. This symbolizes the idea that Rashi's legacy illuminated the name of his hometown throughout the world.

The Jewish community in Germany

From the 4th century, Jews in Germany were valued as merchants who had contacts with communities across Europe. They lived in harmony with non-Jews and were free to practice Judaism. This early woodcut shows a Jewish family rigorously cleaning before the festival of Passover. However, from the 11th century, Christian anti-Judaism led to violence against Jews and communities were driven from city to city. While there was always a Jewish presence in Germany, by the late 15th century, the center of the Jewish world lay in Eastern Europe.

The Jewish community in Britain

Although there were Jews in England by the 11th century, they were expelled by King Edward I in 1290. However, in 1656, a group of Sephardi Jews from the Netherlands, whose families had fled there from Spain in 1492, were able to settle in England. From 1881 onward, there was also a wave of Ashkenazi immigration from Russia. Today, British Jews think of themselves as able and willing to play a full part in British society. This 1920s' photo shows a Jewish boy in London playing at being a bus conductor, complete with ticket punch.

Life in the shtetl
Within the community of the shtetl Jewish law and custom were held in high regard, but towards the end of the 19th century some Jews began to challenge and question this. Marc Chagall (1887–1985) grew up in a shtetl in Russia during this period and became famous as an artist after he moved to Paris. Yet his early paintings, such as *Over Vitebsk*, 1914, recall and reflect on shtetl life with affection, and include flying, dreamlike characters.

THE WORLD OF THE SHTETL

SHTETL IS THE YIDDISH WORD for a small town or village in Eastern Europe and Russia, or a Jewish section within a town where everyone else was Christian. The world of the shtetl began to disappear in the modern age, and was wiped out by Nazi occupation during the Holocaust. Life in a shtetl was one of poverty and hardship but also one of warm family life, strong community feeling, and deep religious devotion. Many who lived in a shtetl look back on it with great affection.

Pale of Settlement
There was strong feeling against Jews in Russian cities, and so Catherine the Great decided to move them out. In 1791, she created the Pale of Settlement as an area where 90 percent of Russian Jews were forced to live. There was heavy discrimination—Jews paid double taxes, were forbidden to have higher education or lease land, and suffered violent attacks. Although many tried to leave, the Pale still had more than five million Jews in 1910. The Russian revolution of 1917 brought the Pale to an end.

Pale of Settlement

☐ Pale of Settlement

Baltic Sea
○ St. Petersburg
○ Moscow
RUSSIAN EMPIRE
THE PALE
Brody ○
○ Kiev
○ Nikolaev
Sebastopol ○○ Yalta
Black Sea

0 km   500   1,000
0 miles   500

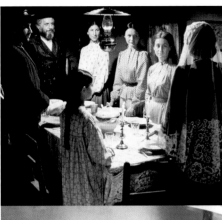

"Good Sabbath!"

The rhythm of the shtetl week centered around the Jewish Sabbath, from sunset on Friday to sunset on Saturday—a day of rest that begins with the mother lighting candles to spread light and love through the home. The Yiddish greeting *Gut Shabbes!* means "Have a good Sabbath!" This scene from *Fiddler on the Roof* shows a typical Sabbath scene.

The classroom

Heder is Hebrew and Yiddish for "room" but refers specifically to the classroom where Jewish boys—and sometimes girls—received a formal Jewish education, alongside what they learned at home. Going to *heder* involved learning to read Hebrew and studying the Torah and other traditional texts, as these boys are doing.

Street scene

Restrictions placed on Jews meant that most could only work in crafts, such as tailoring, or as traders and peddlers. Often the whole family worked to make a living and in the hope of being able to buy a chicken or fish for the Sabbath. The only place where Jews and Christians would usually meet was the market. This photo from 1916 shows two Jewish men carrying water in a shtetl in Poland.

The role of the synagogue

The hub of a shtetl was the *shul*—the Yiddish word for synagogue, the Jewish community center. It is a place for daily prayer, for Jewish study, and for social gatherings, such as weddings. Many *shuls* were simple but, when or if a community could afford to, it created an ornate building—like this *shul* in Poland, which was derelict after the Holocaust but has now been restored.

Hasidism

A new movement emerged in Eastern Europe during the 18th century, a new way of being Jewish. It was inspired by the rabbi Baal Schem Tov, nicknamed the *Besht*—Master of the Good Name. He called his followers Hasidim—the pious. He was against dry book learning and in favor of Jews expressing their joy and devotion to God through singing and dancing ecstatically, like these Hasidim.

VOICES
LIFE IN THE SHTETL

For centuries Jews lived across Russia and Eastern Europe in small towns and villages known as shtetls. Although there had been periods of anti-Semitism, for years most Jews had lived peacefully with no ill will from their Christian neighbors. But eventually the anti-Semitism resurfaced and Jews were again subjected to discrimination. Here, people recall their childhood memories.

"*When I was a young boy, life was very beautiful for us. It was a religious little town and most of the Jews, their whole life revolved around the synagogue. So that means in the morning, early in the morning, when we got up about 4 o'clock or 5 o'clock in the morning we went to heder and from heder we came home and had breakfast and then we went to the normal school, which was with everybody, non-Jews as well as Jews. It was a very, very nice little community. And, after we came back from school, we went back to heder until late in the evening. So that was life when I was a young boy...*"

"*The Gentiles used to wonder at us because we cared so much about religious things—about food and Sabbath and teaching the children Hebrew. They were angry with us for our obstinacy, as they called it, and mocked us and ridiculed the most sacred things. There were wise Gentiles who understood. They were always respectful and openly admired some of our ways. But most of the Gentiles were ignorant. There was one thing, however, the Gentiles always understood, and that was money. They would take any kind of bribe. Peace cost so much a year, in Polotsk. If you did not keep on good terms with your Gentile neighbors, they had a hundred ways of molesting you. If you chased their pigs when they came rooting up your garden, or objected to their children maltreating your children, they might complain against you to the police, stuffing their case with false accusations. If you had not made friends with the police, the case might go to court; and there you lost before the trial began unless the judge had reason to befriend you.*"

Mary Antin
(Born in Russia, 1881)
After the assassination of Alexander II in 1881, her family experienced several pogroms in Russia. They eventually settled in the US.

Peter Hersch
(Born in Czechoslovakia, 1930)
Peter had a happy childhood but later lost all his family except for his sister in the Holocaust.

"*Jasionowka was a little town like thousands and thousands of other towns in Eastern Europe in the Pale of Settlement. In Yiddish it was called shtetl and I think it was the Jewish author Shalom Aleihem who described, he said, 'If you want to know what the map of Eastern Europe looked like in the shtetlach,' he says, 'consider a Friday night challah with poppy seeds sprinkled all over.' That's how those towns were sprinkled over Eastern Europe. ....Jasionowka had no electricity, no paved streets. The homes were not much more than huts, many of them with dirt floors, some of them with wooden floors. We had no running water. Water had to be carried from a well, wood had to be chopped and brought in in order to heat and cook with, and life was extremely hard. How in the world my mother managed to raise eight children and keep them all fed and clothed, to this day, I cannot understand it...It was a very wonderful childhood, and I think the security and joy that I took with me from my childhood is really what managed to get me through the Holocaust and the difficult years that followed. I believe if I had not had that strength and that security, I probably would not have survived.*"

"*Early on Friday afternoons, my mother put into a special red pot kidney beans which had already soaked overnight, together with a handful of barley, some onions, a marrow bone and seasoning, as well as a few raw eggs in their shells. I was often sent with the pot to the bakery and patiently instructed to add water to a spot marked inside the pot once I reached the bakery itself. Scores of children on similar errands were streaming towards the same destination. We each gave the baker a few coins and watched him place the pots inside the heated oven where they would cook slowly and evenly overnight. In this way, a hot dish was guaranteed for Shabbat without actually having to build a fire and cook in the home... To my mind as a child and to this day it's still a miracle: as we would come after synagogue, and there by now there would be hundreds of pots out of the oven lying on the ground, I always managed to find the right pot with just the right little chip marks and get the right cholent with the right taste into the right house at the right time.*"

Bernard Schuster
(Born in Poland, 1928)
Bernard went into hiding during the war and lost many members of his family in the Holocaust.

Hugo Gryn
(Born in Czechoslovakia, 1930)
Hugo's family was sent to Auschwitz, but he and his mother survived. He later became a rabbi.

ENLIGHTENMENT AND EMANCIPATION

The Age of Enlightenment
In the 15th and 16th centuries, Europeans began to question traditional beliefs and challenge Church teachings. Freedom of speech and thought was all. In this painting from 1795, English artist William Blake shows the great scientist Isaac Newton, in the style of religious art, as cosmic designer.

WHEN THE MIDDLE AGES CAME TO AN END, there was a new mood in Europe. Advances in science and technology changed people's lives, and voyages of discovery made Europeans aware of other cultures in various parts of the world. People looked back on earlier centuries as the Dark Ages and believed that they were now in a time of enlightenment and emancipation, when so many possibilities lay before them.

The French Revolution
The slogan on this banner from the French Revolution in 1789, reads "Liberty, fraternity, and equality—or death." This refers to the time when the king and the aristocrats were overthrown and France became the first republic in Europe. It was based on the "rights of man and of the citizen."

Positive portrayal
This 1779 play by Gotthold Ephraim Lessing, a German Christian, explores religious tolerance, and questions whether anyone can know the truth with absolute certainty. The main character is Jewish and is portrayed in a positive way, which was extremely rare in European literature, art, and drama. Lessing probably based *Nathan the Wise* on Moses Mendelsohn, a Jewish friend.

Reform Judaism
The Dohany Street synagogue in Budapest, Hungary, is typical of the style of Neolog or Reform synagogues. It is grand, confident, and modern for its time. Reform Judaism began in Germany in 1800 as a way of helping modern Jews to be both modern and traditional in the way that they practiced Judaism. It did this by concentrating on what were essential Jewish beliefs and values.

Emancipation of Europe

Emancipation before 1800
Emancipation between 1800 and 1850
Emancipation between 1850 and 1900
Emancipation after 1900

Political emancipation

Following the French Revolution, every Jew in France was given equality with other French citizens, as long as they promised to be loyal to the State and the Jewish community did not expect to be recognized as different from any other. The Edict of Tolerance in Germany made similar promises. Gradually, Jews across Europe were given political emancipation—the freedom to be full citizens.

NORWAY
1851

SWEDEN
1865

GREAT BRITAIN
1890

DENMARK
1848

NETHERLANDS
1796

PRUSSIA
1850

RUSSIA
1917

BELGIUM
1830

GERMANY
1871

FRANCE
1789

SWITZERLAND
1874

AUSTRIA-HUNGARY
1867

° Bordeaux

○ Avignon

PORTUGAL
1910

SPAIN
1930

ROMANIA
1918

SERBIA
1878

BULGARIA
1878

ITALY
1848–1870

THE OTTOMAN EMPIRE
1908

0 km   500   1,000   1,500
0 miles   500   1,000

The dream of Zion

Because Jews still experienced prejudice in everyday life, some felt that they could only be equal and free in their ancient homeland, Zion—another name for Jerusalem or Israel. Pioneering Zionists, like these men and women, made their way to the homeland from 1881 onward. They worked hard at fulfilling the ancient dream to "make the desert bloom."

Land and language

This modern Israeli stamp bears the image of Ben Yehudah, the father of modern Hebrew. Born in Lithuania in the 19th century, he and his wife emigrated to Palestine in 1881. Believing that a nation living in its own land should speak its own language, he revived spoken Hebrew and introduced modern words.

ISRAEL   250

Enlightenment in Eastern Europe

By the late 19th century, enlightenment ideas of Western Europe had reached Eastern Europe and Russia, influencing the *haskalah*—the Jewish enlightenment movement. Secular education for Jews was now possible and was considered a great benefit. An important center of *haskalah* was Odessa, Russia, where this family lived—reading a Russian newspaper would never have happened before the *haskalah*.

JEWISH LIFE IN EUROPE

IN THE MIDDLE AGES, European leaders allowed Jews to settle in their lands, and even encouraged Jewish settlers when they needed their skills. A few worked at the courts of nobles as musicians, diplomats, or interpreters. Toward the end of the 18th century, many European countries began to abolish laws that discriminated against Jews, a period known as the Emancipation, and Jews were able to take part in more aspects of European society.

Jews in the Middle Ages
The medieval Church did not allow Jews to own land or hold some occupations. It also forbade Christians to lend money with interest, but not to borrow money. So Christians used Jews as moneylenders, as this 15th-century German woodcut shows.

In the 1930s there were almost 10 million Jews in Europe.

Jews in trade and industry
In the modern age, Jews were able to move into bigger business. Some became familiar household names. Michael Marks (1859–1907) was a poor Russian emigrant to England who started as a peddler, went on to have a market stall, and gradually built up the large chain of stores now known as "Marks & Spencer." Today the Marks family has large charitable foundations.

Literature
Jews are often called "The People of the Book," because they have always valued language, from study of the Torah to humor, poetry, and storytelling. One important Jewish novelist was Franz Kafka (1883–1924), a Czech author, who wrote about people who are confused by life. His most famous work is called *Metamorphosis*.

Science and medicine
In medieval Europe, Jews made up 1 percent of the population, yet 50 percent of doctors were Jewish. Today, many Jews work in medicine and other areas of science. Many have been awarded the Nobel Prize for science, including German-born Albert Einstein (1879–1955). It was Einstein who established the International Rescue Committee to aid victims of Nazism in 1933.

Jewish population in Europe 1933

- ■ 1,000,000 and over
- ■ 500,000–999,999
- ■ 100,000–499,000
- □ 10,000–99,999
- □ 0–9,999

Jewish settlement

Throughout the Middle Ages, Jewish people moved to escape outbursts of violence, or were expelled from one land to another. In modern times, too, some Jews have moved to places of greater safety or better opportunities. In 1933, most Jews lived in Eastern Europe, especially Poland and the Soviet Union (now Russia). These were communities of some of the most traditional and religiously observant Jews in Europe.

NORWAY 1,500
SWEDEN 6,500
FINLAND 1,800
ESTONIA 5,000
IRELAND 3,600
GREAT BRITAIN 300,000
DENMARK 6,000
LATVIA 95,000
DANZIG 9,200
LITHUANIA 155,000
SOVIET UNION 3,020,000
NETHERLANDS 160,000
GERMANY 565,000
POLAND 3,000,000
BELGIUM 60,000
LUXEMBOURG 2,200
FRANCE 225,000
CZECHOSLOVAKIA 357,000
SWITZERLAND 18,000
AUSTRIA 250,000
HUNGARY 445,000
ROMANIA 760,000
PORTUGAL 1,000
SPAIN 4,000
ITALY 48,000
YUGOSLAVIA 70,000
BULGARIA 50,000
ALBANIA 200
EUROPEAN TURKEY 56,000
GREECE 100,000

0 km   500   1,000   1,500
0 miles   500   1,000

Music and drama

Music has always played a large part in Jewish culture. Since the 1800s, there have been many Jewish composers and musicians, including Polish-born pianist Arthur Rubinstein (1887–1982). There have also been reknowned Jewish actors, directors, and producers of film and theater.

The arts

Traditionally, Jewish art was limited to creating objects used in worship and illustrating texts, but never depicted people. Modern Jewish artists, however, have portrayed people in both sculpture and painting, like this figure by Italian Amedeo Modigliani (1884–1920).

Psychoanalysis

Sigmund Freud (1856–1939), an Austrian Jew, has been called "the father of psychoanalysis," because of his revolutionary work in the study of the mind. In this work, he explored a patient's feelings and behavior by interpreting their dreams and use of language.

Politics

Once no longer banned from public life, many Jews became involved in politics. Rosa Luxemburg (1870–1919) was one of the most famous Jewish women in politics. A leader of the Polish social democratic movement, she supported the use of strikes to achieve social change.

23

Ecclesia and Synagoga

This window, from the 13th-century church at Marburg in Germany, reveals the early belief tha Christianity was superior to Judaism. Christianity represented by Ecclesia, is on the left and Judaisr or Synagoga, on the right. While Ecclesia wears crown, Synagoga is blindfolded, refusing to see t truth, and holds a goat's horns, symbol of the dev

Malicious rumors about Jews

For centuries European folklore demonizec Jews, portraying them with horns and fork tails, or as reptiles. However, the charge th caused the greatest fear was the "blood libe shown in this medieval woodcut. This was the claim that Jews killed Christian babies for their blood, to make special bread.

THE HISTORY OF ANTI-SEMITISM

ANTI-SEMITISM, THE HATRED OF JEWS, dates from ancient times but was strengthened by the medieval Church, which taught that Jews were to blame for the death of Christ. Along with Christian beliefs came folk ideas of Jews as evil. Although now seen for what they are, both traditions have influenced people and politics today.

The Crusades

In 1096, the Pope called on Christians to reclaim the Holy Land from Islamic contro and Crusaders set off across Europe, fired

Pogroms

The word pogrom comes from the Russian for "devastation" and is the name for the organized massacres of Jews that took place in Russia and Eastern Europe from the 17th century. As recently as 1905, about 3,000 Jews were murdered in some 600 pogroms. This father runs from his burning shtetl with his child.

LE PÉRIL JUIF

LES PROTOCOLES DES SAGES DE SION

A Jewish conspiracy

The *Protocols of the Elders of Zion* is a book claiming to contain notes of meetings between Jewish leaders plotting to conquer and control the world, as this cover shows. Although a hoax, it is still published today by anti-Semitic groups. This is a French edition from the 1890s.

The Dreyfus Affair

In 1894, Alfred Dreyfus, a Jewish officer in the French army, was arrested for spying. This poster calls Dreyfus a traitor, yet there was no real evidence against him. Despite this, the trial continued and Dreyfus was found guilty. The case caused a political scandal, and exposed anti-Semitism in France. Eventually the verdict against Dreyfus was overturned.

MUSÉE DES HORREURS — n:6 — le Traître!

Theodor Herzl and Zionism

Herzl was an Austro-Hungarian reporter covering the Dreyfus trial. Shocked by the open anti-Semitism of the court, and in France, he concluded that Jews could never be free in Europe and needed a land of their own—the idea of Zionism. In 1896, Herzl organized the first Zionist Congress, to make plans for a Jewish homeland.

Modern anti-Semitism

While there is less anti-Semitism today than in the Middle Ages, or during the Holocaust, it has not disappeared. Lies are still spoken and written about Jews and as a result Jews may suffer discrimination. There is vandalism in Jewish places, such as the desecration of this cemetery, which took place in Herrlisheim, France, in 2004.

"I advise that the Jews' houses also be razed and destroyed. For they pursue in them the same aims as in their synagogues. Instead they might be lodged under a roof or in a barn, like the gypsies. This will bring home to them that they are not masters in our country, as they boast, but that they are living in exile and in captivity, as they incessantly wail and lament about us before God."

Martin Luther, The Jews and Their Lies, *1543*

Jews burnt at the stake, *Nuremberg Chronicle* 1493

NAZI RULE

NAZI RULE BEGAN IN **1933** when Adolf Hitler became leader of Germany, and signaled the end of 14 years of democracy. German laws now became a way of putting the Nazis' racist ideas into practice. Germany aimed to bring all of Europe and eventually all the world under its control. It was a time of terror for non-Nazis, especially those that the Nazis thought were subhuman.

The German Parliament hails the Führer
On March 12, 1938, German forces occupied Austria and annexed it to Germany. The next day, Hitler—known as the Führer, or supreme leader of Germany—convened the German parliament, the *Reichstag*. The members gave him a standing ovation and made the Nazi salute, to show their pride in what Germany had done.

Treaty of Versailles—Britain, the US, France, Italy, and Germany agree the borders of Europe after World War 1

Adolf Hitler becomes leader of the Nazi Party

Beer Hall Putsch—Nazis attempt to topple the government but fail and Hitler is imprisoned for treason

After German defeat in World War I, the Kaiser abdicates and Germany is declared a republic

The National Socialist Party, or Nazis, adopt the swastika as their symbol

Benito Mussolini, leader of the Fascist Party, becomes prime minister of Italy

Locarno Pact Conference in Switzerland confirms the German borders. Hitler publishes *Mein Kampf*

EUROPE

| 1914 | 1915 | 1917 | 1918 | 1919 | 1920 | 1921 | 1922 | 1923 | 1925 | 1929 |

WORLD

World War I begins (to 1918)

Revolution in Russia sees the czar abdicate and the Bolsheviks (communists) take over

Russia becomes the Union of Soviet Socialist Republics (USSR), or Soviet Union

The Wall Street Crash—the collapse of the New York Stock Exchange—leads to global economic depression

About 1,500,000 Armenians massacred or deported by Turks

British Mandate (administration) of Palestine begins (to 1948). League of Nations created to promote international peace and security

Hitler becomes Chancellor of Germany. Dachau concentration camp set up in Germany to hold political prisoners

In Germany, the Nuremberg Laws outlaw marriage between Jewish and non-Jewish Germans

German troops first move into Austria and then invade the Sudetenland. In Germany, many Jews are killed or wounded in the violence of *Kristallnacht*

The Blitz begins— German planes bomb London and other British cities

Hitler becomes both chancellor and president, to gain total control of Germany

Hitler denounces the Locarno Pact and moves troops into the Rhineland. Olympic Games held in Germany

Germany invades Czechoslovakia and Poland

Germany invades the Soviet Union

1933   1934   1935   1936   1938   1939   1940   1941   1942

World War II begins (to 1945)

Japan bombs ships in Pearl Harbor, Hawaii

First US forces arrive in Europe

THE LEGACY OF THE GREAT WAR

WORLD WAR I (1914–1918) became known as "The Great War" because of its vast scale, its huge impact on nations and individuals, and the extensive damage. Germany suffered heavy casualties, lost land, and had to pay reparations (compensation). This left the economy weak and the people low in spirits. The Nazis gained support by blaming the Jews for the losses and persuading Germans that they would make Germany great again.

"Jew Count"
Christian images on German cards showed the Church's support for the war. Despite Nazi claims that Jews had shirked military service, a "Jew Count" in 1916 showed that a high proportion of Jews had volunteered. More than 100,000 served in the army and 35,000 were decorated for bravery.

THE FORGOTTEN MASSACRES

During World War I the Ottoman (Turkish) Empire fought on Germany's side—and most Turks were Muslim. The Turks accused their Armenian Christian minority of siding with Russia, their enemy. As a result, in 1915 the Turks massacred 1,500,000 Armenian Christians. Turkey disputes this figure and claims that the Armenians simply died in the way of war. This poster (right) was part of an American campaign to provide relief for the Armenian Christians who were forced to flee Turkey. Hitler is reported to have used the Armenian massacres to justify his own policies, saying that since no one remembered the Armenian genocide, no one would care how the Nazis dealt with the "Jewish problem."

Armenian Christians find refuge aboard a French ship

Germany loses The Great War
The region of Lorraine, which Germany and France both claimed as their own, became a battlefield in World War I. These German soldiers, who had once proudly marched off to war, hopeful of victory, have been captured by the French in the Lorraine region. Their faces reveal their sense of national shame.

Treaty of Versailles

The war was ended by the Treaty of Versailles, a peace treaty created by the Allies—Britain, France, Italy, and the US—and signed in 1919, near Paris. The Allies wanted to ensure that Germany could never go to war again and it had to agree to reduce its armies, lose land, and pay crippling reparations. This cartoon expresses Germany's deep sense of humiliation.

The Locarno Pact

In 1925, Britain, France, Italy, Germany, Belgium, Poland, and Czechoslovakia met in Locarno, in Switzerland, to confirm the borders of Europe as agreed to in the Treaty of Versailles. But the question mark on this election poster of 1928 shows there was a feeling it need not be respected. By 1936 Hitler had gone back on the Locarno Pact completely.

During World War I, more than 12,000 German-Jewish soldiers were killed on the battlefield.

SETTING THE STAGE

HITLER KNEW the German people were depressed by their losses in World War I and used their disillusionment for his own aims by blaming "outsiders," meaning communists and Jews. This united the Germans against a common enemy. Hitler also wanted to disrupt meetings of political opponents and protect himself from attacks, so he formed a private army of storm troopers, also known as Brownshirts.

Anti-Semitism
The Nazis played on the fears of ordinary Germans by depicting Jews as controlling, greedy, and cruel. In this poster from 1924, the Star of David identifies the giant wire-puller as Jewish. He is controlling the workers, pulling the strings as if they were his puppets.

Anti-communism
The Nazis also sought to discredit the Social Democratic Party (SPD), which had voted against Nazi laws in 1933. This poster shows an SPD angel, wearing the hammer and sickle symbol of communism, walking hand in hand with a wealthy, capitalist Jew, warning Germans that neither could be trusted.

Hyperinflation
After World War I, the German economy was weak and the cost of living was high. By 1923, inflation—continual increases in prices—was at a staggering rate. Printing more money just made it worthless. Many Germans burned money for heating because it was cheaper than buying fuel. A new currency was introduced in 1924.

Italian Fascism
In 1922, the Fascist Party, under Mussolini, came to power in Italy, emphasizing national unity, military values, and hatred of communism. It was Mussolini's squads of fascist supporters, called Blackshirts, that inspired Hitler to form his own private army of Brownshirts (above).

In the 1928 elections, less than three percent of Germans voted for the Nazi party.

Political speeches

Hitler was drawn to the German Workers' Party, but suggested changing the name to the National Socialist German Workers Party—the *Nationalsozialistishe Deutsche Arbeiterpartei* or Nazis. Although socialism stressed equality, Hitler added "national" to mean that only Germans were equal. He was often invited to give political speeches because of his power to stir up people's hatred, and is depicted here addressing the crowd in a beer hall.

The Munich Beer Hall Putsch

In 1923, Hitler decided on a *Putsch*—a sudden and illegal use of force—to overthrow the government. Armed storm troopers led by Hitler burst into a government meeting. Hitler fired shots in the air and declared the start of the National Revolution. Other Nazi leaders seized the war ministry, arresting Jews and political opponents. The next day Hitler and 3,000 Nazi supporters marched through Munich before police stopped them.

MY STRUGGLE

After the Nazi march in Munich, Hitler was captured and charged with high treason. Although he was found guilty, he received the minimum sentence of five years in prison. There he began writing his ideas about the evils of Jews and communists, the connections between them, and what could be done. These ideas were published in 1925 in Hitler's book *Mein Kampf* (My Struggle). Five million copies were published by 1939. Millions more have been published since and the book has been translated into many languages.

ADOLF HITLER

MEIN KAMPF

(MON COMBAT)

L'ANTISEMITISME
L'ANTI-MARXISME
LE RACISME
L'ANSCHLUSS

15 f.

POPULAR SUPPORT

AT FIRST THERE WAS LITTLE SUPPORT for the Nazis in Germany, but they learned the powerful appeal of uniforms, symbols, rallies, and salutes from the experience of the Italian Fascists. Nazi theories of race also helped to make ordinary Germans feel superior and strengthened popular support. Gradually, the Nazis increased their appeal, especially with young people.

Children and young people

The Nazis used youth movements to influence Germans at an impressionable age, and joining a youth movement became almost compulsory. Children wore uniforms and took part in activities that emphasized discipline and fitness, with tests of endurance and self-sacrifice. This girl is collecting money for youth hostels and homes.

Theories of race

Posters like this were hung on German classroom walls as an aid to education. The Nazis drew on 19th-century theories that people could be divided into separate races, some superior and some inferior. The "master races" were the Northern Europeans, especially the Germans, who they claimed were descended from Aryans, the first people of ancient India.

The Hitler salute

The Nazi salute was a sign of loyalty to Hitler. It was modeled on the salute of the Italian Fascists, the ancient Romans, as well as the ancient Germans. It showed a warlike spirit, with the arm resembling a raised spear. Nazi supporters would salute and greet each other, and at mass gatherings like this youth rally, would proclaim *"Sieg Heil!"* meaning "Victory and Hail."

The Nazi flag

Hitler designed the Nazi flag. He chose red, black, and white, the historical colors of Germany's flag, as a sign that democracy and the Weimar Republic were over. Red stood for the social idea of Nazism, white for nationalism, and the black swastika for the struggle of the Aryan man. At this 1933 rally in Nuremberg, members of the SS carry the flags as standards.

Es lebe Deutschland!

THE SWASTIKA

Eine schlägt auch für uns

In 1920, the Nazis adopted the symbol of the hooked cross, an ancient German symbol for the god of thunder. It was similar to the swastika, an Indian sign of goodness, which was appropriate since the Aryan race originated in India. The swastika appeared in Nazi insignia and even on everyday items, such as this clock.

The cult of Hitler

In this poster, Hitler is depicted in the same way that Jesus is often portrayed at his baptism—with a powerful spiritual light in the sky and a dove hovering overhead. This was typical of the growing cult in which Hitler was treated as a god. Many Germans believed that he had supernatural powers, and some addressed prayers to him if they were worried or unhappy. This poster declares "Long live Germany!"

In 1938, Hitler was Time magazine's man of the year.

IN BY THE BACK DOOR

HITLER'S ACCURATE PREDICTION of the Great Depression that began in the US in 1929 led people to believe he could help Germany's economy. The Nazis then used the tripling of German unemployment in 1930 to win support for their plans for a confident, independent Germany. However, not everyone was convinced, so Hitler resorted to other methods to gain total power.

Election campaigner during the German presidential election, 1932

DATE	NAZI SHARE OF VOTES	DEPUTIES ELECTED	VOTES IN MILLIONS
May 20, 1928	2.6%	12	0.81
September 14, 1930	18.3%	107	6.41
July 31, 1932	37.3%	230	13.75
November 6, 1932	33.1%	196	11.74
March 5, 1933	43.9%	288	17.28

Wall Street Crash
In 1929, when New York stockbrokers in the Wall Street Stock Exchange called in loans, the value of stocks fell. In panic, Americans closed their bank accounts and the Stock Exchange collapsed. The German and American economies were closely linked, so Germans were also affected.

Nazi election victories
The Nazis were slow to win votes and get deputies elected to the government, as the chart above shows. In fact, in 1932 support dipped. The Nazis never won an outright majority, even in 1933 when they came to power.

Hitler becomes chancellor
After the 1932 elections, president Paul von Hindenburg refused Hitler's request to be made chancellor, afraid that Hitler would be dictatorial. But in January 1933, the Conservative parties supported Hitler, hoping to use him to their advantage. The president finally agreed. Hitler immediately took over all the functions of state, making Germany a dictatorship. To increase popular support, Hitler organized huge rallies, like this torchlight procession in Berlin.

The burning of the Reichstag

Since Hitler could not be certain that he would win an election, he used other means to achieve his goals. As he hoped, horrified crowds gathered when the parliament building, the Reichstag, mysteriously caught fire. A communist caught with matches was forced to confess. As a result, Hitler was able to adopt emergency powers to ban socialists and communists from the elections.

PERIODS OF GERMAN GOVERNMENT

The First Reich: The Holy Roman Empire	843–1806
The Second Reich: The German Empire	1871–1919
The Weimar Republic: A democratic government	1919–1933
The Third Reich	1933–1945

One People, One Empire, One Leader

Inspired by Mussolini's title *il Duce*—the Duke, Hitler took the title of *der Führer*—the Leader. He expected to be addressed as *Mein Führer*, My Leader. This propaganda poster declares "One People, One Empire, One Leader," a slogan that aimed to make Hitler an icon of unity.

The beginning of the Third Reich

Hitler wanted to make laws without the interference of parliament, so he proposed the Enabling Act. Storm troopers outside the parliament building ensured the law was passed. Hitler now had a legal right to be a dictator. When the president died in 1934 Hitler became both chancellor and president—he had gained total control.

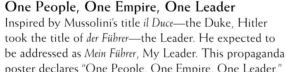

THE AUTOBAHNS

Hitler dreamed of a German superhighway network that would be the best in the world, and a milestone in the building up of the German people. Here, in September 1933, he is seen ceremonially digging the foundation of an *Autobahn*, or highway. Good roads were a great advantage to the German people and increased Hitler's popularity. They had symbolic value as a sign of German achievement and collective effort. They also signaled that all Germans were connected, quite literally, and so the country was united.

Ein Volk, ein Reich, ein Führer!

"I had been skating that day … when I got home …
we heard that Hitler had become Chancellor.
Everybody shook. As kids of ten we shook."

Leslie Frankel recalls hearing the news that Hitler had become Chancellor of Germany

VOICES
NAZI GERMANY

When Hitler came to power in 1933, nobody could have foreseen the horrors that lay ahead, even though people were alarmed at the increasing climate of anti-Semitism in Germany. However, many Jews decided not to flee because they did not want to leave their homes and thought the situation would pass.

" *IN 1935, WHEN Hitler was already very much in control and had become Chancellor, I went to Cologne to meet some of my old college friends. Then I went to Berlin and went to see the woman in charge of the Jewish community. She gave me the information that I wanted and before I went, the sight of all those flags, the blood red flag, you know, with the swastika, struck terror, really terror into me. And you never knew when you'd be picked up! I was very scared on the train, especially at the borders. But fortunately I got through and then, as I sat with this woman, she said, 'You're an American, you can get out of here, we can't, no country wants us. You can get out. Go out. Go out and scream! Scream so the whole world will know what we're suffering here. Just get out.' So I left and I went to Poland.* "

Ruth Gruber
(Born in New York, 1911)
Ruth was at the University of Cologne from 1931–32. Here she recalls her visit in 1935.

"I WENT TO Germany to look up some of our old friends and families and the stories I heard all over Germany from the Jewish people—were just terrible. It wasn't even as bad as it was in later years, but everybody was concerned about what was happening. A lot of people wanted to get out of Germany, but they said, 'Well, my mother's here and my father's here and they're old and we don't want to leave them. We have our business here and we don't want to leave our business.' I suggested to many of them that it was a good time to leave Germany because, as an outsider, I had a better picture of what was going on. What disturbed me most is that Germany was in the midst of rearming! Everything was in armament. Every person was in uniform. Tanks were on the streets and there were parades and loudspeakers…and everybody was singing Deutschland Über Alles and Heute Deutschland Morgen die Welt, you know, Today Germany, Tomorrow the World, and there was a strange spirit of nationalism. And of course the situation for the Jews was getting worse, although a lot felt that the problem was temporary and would eventually go away. It didn't go away, as we all know, and I left Germany. I have a note from a series of talks I gave after I came home in which I said, 'There is absolutely no future for any Jews in Germany. I think the Jews have to get out of there.' But nobody was listening."

"THE REAL SERIOUS change that I noticed was when we found one morning, when we went to school, that all the other children had formed two lines in front of the school house door and as we walked through those two lines they beat us up! I went to the teacher and I complained and he said, 'Well, what did you expect you dirty Jew?' And from that we figured that he had the children every morning in church (they had to go for mass every morning) and we figured that what he had done is organized the children to beat us up."

Emma Mogilensky
(Born in Germany, 1923)
Emma was just fifteen years old when she experienced the anti-Semitism she describes here.

Fred Baer
(Born in Germany, 1910)
Fred's family went to the United States before the war started. He recalls the reluctance of the Jews to leave.

THE THIRD REICH

HITLER'S REGIME was called the Third Reich—or Third Empire. It began as a police state but increasingly controlled people's actions and thoughts. The *Schutzstaffel*, or SS, started in the 1920s as Hitler's personal guards but, after 1933, it became a second army. The Secret State Police, the Gestapo, also had great power and tortured people who had been arrested without charge.

Hitler the flag bearer
By the time of the Third Reich, there were more pictures of Hitler than of anyone else in history. The idea was to fill people's minds with his image, and in some pictures Hitler appears as a religious or folk icon. This famous painting from 1938, by Austrian artist Hubert Lanzinger, is called *The Flag Bearer* and portrays Hitler as a knight.

Dachau concentration camp
Dachau was one of the first concentration camps in Germany, dating from 1933. It held 1,200 inmates, mostly political prisoners. Conditions were not as harsh as in later camps, but many died from the poor conditions or were killed for breaking a camp rule.

The Nuremberg Laws

With the Third Reich in power, relationships between Jews and non-Jews were often mocked in public. Some people were made to wear placards saying that they were a "Jewish pig" or were marrying a "Jewish pig." In 1935, anti-Semitism was legalized in two Nuremberg Laws. One made marriage between Jews and non-Jews illegal to protect German "racial purity" and the other stated that only "pure" Germans were Reich citizens.

Land-grabbing

Hitler was determined to make Germany a great power again that could dominate Europe. *Lebensraum*, meaning "living space", was a Nazi term for land-grabbing. As this map shows, this began with Austria in 1938. Hitler planned to unite all German-speakers in one country and create a "Greater Germany", which would expand eastwards.

Into Austria

Hitler urged Austrian Nazis to demand that Austria and Germany be united. Then, in March 1938, the German army invaded Austria. This parade in Innsbruck was held the next day, after the Austrian troops were sworn into the Third Reich. The *Anschluss* (political union) was complete.

The Sudetenland

The *Anschluss* strengthened Germany's drive for more land. German speakers in the Sudetenland, a region of Czechoslovakia wanted to join Greater Germany and Hitler claimed that, by invading the Sudetenland, he was freeing them. As the troops marched in, locals had to salute. Then in 1939 Hitler invaded Czechoslovakia from the Sudetenland.

NAZI PROPAGANDA

IN HIS BOOK *MEIN KAMPF*, Hitler wrote that the use of emotion, rather than reason, would convince people to share Nazi beliefs. The Minister for Propaganda, Joseph Goebbels, promoted Nazi ideals in an emotional way to influence people's thoughts. Everything the Third Reich communicated had a political message, from speeches and posters to films and architecture.

Nazi "heroes"

The Nazis wanted people to perceive them as heroes, able to attack evil and protect Germany from harm. In this poster, the Nazi figure is depicted as a brave warrior. Many propaganda posters adapted imagery from Christian legends and European folklore.

Art and architecture

Hitler banned, hid, or destroyed modern art because he believed it was corrupt. Instead, he promoted great painters of the past and commissioned new work in traditional styles. The architect Albert Speer rewarded Hitler's friendship by designing imposing buildings, such as this grandstand at the Nazi Party rally grounds in Nuremberg.

Hitler as savior

To record the 1934 Nazi Party Congress, Hitler commissioned a propaganda movie called *Triumph of the Will*. Its theme was the return of Germany as a great power and Hitler as a German savior bringing the nation glory. The movie director, Leni Riefenstahl, used clever techniques, such as this shot placing Hitler in line with the church but in the foreground so that he appears to tower over it.

Within days of becoming chancellor, Hitler closed down the printing presses of all organizations that opposed him.

Children, church, kitchen

The ideals that the Nazis glorified for women were *Kinder, Kirche, Küche*, which means children, church, kitchen. Family images such as this were meant to motivate women to strive for these goals. White, non-Jewish women were encouraged to have large families in order to produce soldiers and workers, and expand the Aryan population.

Selective breeding

This poster claims that "God cannot want the sick and ailing to reproduce." It aimed to persuade people that sterilization was necessary to prevent the birth of babies with illnesses or disabilities. In later years, sterilization would be replaced by the outright killing of "undesirables," including races that the Nazis believed were inferior.

--denn Gott kann nicht wollen, daß Kranke und Sieche sich in Kranken und Siechen fortpflanzen

Forbidden friendships

During the 1920s in Germany there were about 250,000 black people as well as other minority groups, such as Jews and Romanies. The Nazis claimed that all these people were *Untermenschen*, or subhumans, and polluted the country. This photograph depicts a friendship between a white, non-Jewish woman and a black woman. The relationship is discouraged with the caption "A loss of racial pride."

Das Ergebnis!

Der Raſſeſtolz ſchwindet.

Victimized groups

In this Nazi filmstrip, links are made between stereotyped images of "subhumans," including Arabs, Asians, and Africans. Joining these people and shown very large is a stereotypical Jew. By visually connecting these demonized groups, the Nazi belief that they are guilty people is reinforced in the minds of their target audience—white, non-Jewish Germans. The caption on this poster reads "The Jew is a bastard."

Orientalen Neger Vorderaſiaten Hamiten

Der Jude iſt ein Baſtard.

THE RISE OF ANTI-SEMITISM

JEWS LIVED in permanent fear during the Nazi period. Law after law was passed to deprive them of their rights and restrict their lives. Most non-Jewish Germans turned against the Jews living in their local communities, and violent outbursts were frequent. However, a large proportion of German Jews did not leave the country because they believed the situation would not last and Germany was their home.

Burning books

Just as the Nazis destroyed any art that they considered to be immoral or "un-German," they also burned books—many of them by Jewish authors. Bonfires such as this one near the Berlin Opera House were a spectacle for the public to watch, and reinforced hatred of the writers.

Public humiliations

Nazis attacked and humiliated Jews in many ways, such as by pulling hair from men's beards or forcing them to dance in public. Jews were also made to scrub the streets, as shown here in Vienna, while Austrian Nazis and local residents watched.

"Night of Broken Glass"

On November 9, 1938, Joseph Goebbels, Hitler's Propaganda Minister, organized attacks on Jews in Germany, Sudetenland, and Austria. Known as *Kristallnacht* (Night of Broken Glass), 96 Jews died and hundreds were wounded. More than 1,000 synagogues and 7,500 Jewish businesses were destroyed. Jews had to pay huge sums to repair the damage and 30,000 of them were sent to concentration camps.

Stereotypes of Jews

German children were shown anti-Semitic ideas and images from an early age. The Jew as a kidnapper in this storybook played on their fears. Other stereotypes of Jews were as money-grabbing cheats, monsters, and slimy creepy-crawlies. In time, the images themselves became codes for "Jew."

Anti-Semitic laws

Between 1933 and 1939, German Jews lost almost all of their civil rights and were singled out for persecution. Eventually, in Germany and Nazi-occupied regions, Jews were forced to show on their clothing that they were Jewish. In some places this was through a Star of David patch, in others an armband.

1933

Jews no longer allowed to work as lawyers, judges, or civil servants. Jewish children often forbidden from playing with other children.

1935

Jewish writers, musicians, and art dealers forbidden from working. Jews only allowed to sit on public benches marked "For Jews."

1936

Jews had to hand over their bicycles and typewriters. Jewish vets forced to stop working. Jewish converts to Christianity classed as Jewish.

1938

Jewish doctors and midwives forced to stop working. Jews no longer allowed to have their own businesses. Jews forbidden to attend the movies, theater, opera, concerts, or swimming pools. Jewish children expelled from German schools.

1939

Jews forced to hand over their valuables to the police. Jews evicted from their homes without reason or notice. Jews not allowed out after 8 p.m. in the winter and 9 p.m. in the summer.

In 1938, 18,000 Polish Jews were expelled from Germany overnight.

Revival of old fears

The popular Nazi newspaper *Der Stürmer* often published anti-Semitic articles. This 1934 edition promoted the idea of a Jewish conspiracy by showing Jews faking their loyalty to Germany. The paper also featured stories about a religious ritual that Jews had been falsely charged with centuries before, that of draining the blood of Christians.

"J" for Jew

This passport belonged to a young Jewish woman called Edith Baum. Every Jew had to have their passport clearly stamped with the letter "J." On passports and other documents, Jewish men had to add the name "Israel" and Jewish women the name "Sarah." These additions were aimed at making it impossible for Jews to hide their identity.

Assimilated German Jews

In the 19th century, Germany became a safe and comfortable place for Jews and many had prospered, feeling fully "German." Some stopped practicing their religion and some converted to Christianity. This German Jewish family looks like any other German family, but it was assimilated Jews such as these that the Nazis found most worrying.

A synagogue on fire in Bielefeld, Germany, during the Night of Broken Glass, November 9, 1938

"While I was traveling to Dinslaken I heard in the train that anti-Semitic riots had broken out everywhere, and that many Jews had been arrested. Synagogues everywhere are burning."

Yitzhak S. Herz recalls the terror of Kristallnacht while he was

VOICES
JEWS UNDER THE NAZIS

The Nazis introduced many laws to discriminate against Jews and deprive them of their rights. Then, on *Kristallnacht*, November 9–10, 1938, synagogues and Jewish businesses were destroyed by soldiers and ordinary citizens. Later, Jews were forced to carry identification—in the form of new ID cards—and also to wear a yellow star on their clothes, marking them out as Jewish.

"WE SAW THEM starting to march on the streets, and, of course, the next day, all the stores already had signs saying, 'Juden sind hier unerwunscht' ('Jews are not wanted here'). And the Jewish stores, you know, 'Jude,' they wrote on them and all kinds of things happened. There were a lot of things going on and you were sitting there and you didn't really know what was going to happen—and soon we found out. It was terrible. The first thing that I remember very well, when I came home from school, (this was just in the beginning), I went on the street where we lived and there was a whole bunch of people standing around shouting and shouting, 'Juden!' and so on and so forth, and here I see my mother on the street, on her feet, cleaning the street! They took her to clean up the signs that they put on the streets for the election. And I said, 'Ma! What are you doing here?' And she said, 'Thea, go home! Go home!' She didn't want me to stay there. And I cried tremendously and I didn't go home, I stayed there saying, 'Mommy, Mommy!' And the people, they had no compassion whatsoever. They were full of hate. All of them. All of them."

"IN THE WINTER they came and picked up my father and mother, and then us too, to shovel the snow. We had to shovel snow for hours. And the people were standing around laughing. I remember I had a pair of boots and they wanted them... They didn't take them, but I was afraid I would have to go barefoot in the snow."

Thea Rumstein
(Born in Austria, 1928)
Thea recalls some early anti-Semitic attacks on her family before they were all deported to Theresienstadt ghetto.

"*T*HERE WAS A big table there in the entry of the City Hall and people that I used to see on the street, that I knew, were there and signing us up because we had to have new identification cards. Everyone in Europe always had, and in France always had, like we have here, a social security card or a driver's license as an identification card. We just had an identification card with where you live, where you were born, if you were a student or working, or whatever. And then on that same card they changed it and they gave it another color. Instead of being beige like before, it was a yellow one and across was a stamp, and it said 'Juif' on it, 'Jew,' and it was like you brand an animal—that's how I felt."

"*I*WAS SO upset! I can't tell you. I went over to my girlfriend's, who we sat together in the school years and the mother opened the door and she said, 'I heard you were a bloody pig, a Jewish pig. Don't come here again!' and threw the door in my face. I stood there like an ox! I couldn't understand what had happened! My best girlfriend's mother, she looked after me as if I was her child—from one day to the other she changed."

"*O*N NOVEMBER 10, 1938, in the morning, we went out to school and suddenly we saw smoke and fire and temples. They had started a pogrom in Berlin and started breaking windows. They broke the windows of all the Jewish stores and took the merchandise. They brought big, big picket signs that said, 'Don't buy from the Jews!' and they started burning the synagogues."

Michelle Cohen-Rodriguez
(Born in France, 1935)
Michelle recalls the degradation she felt when forced to carry a Jewish identification card.

Sigi Hart
(Born in Germany, 1925)
Sigi recalls *Kristallnacht* in 1938, when Jewish stores and synagogues were smashed and burned.

Leonie Hilton
(Born in Germany, 1916)
Leonie relates her shock and dismay when her best friend's mother no longer accepted her.

VICTIMS OF NAZISM

THE NAZIS BELIEVED a wide range of people were inferior to them and had no place in Germany or even the world. They believed in the survival of the fittest, with the strong having rights over the weak. In particular, the Nazis wanted to destroy two groups who would neither change or be "cured"—the Jews and the Romanies. Though often called "gypsies," Romanies found this name an insult.

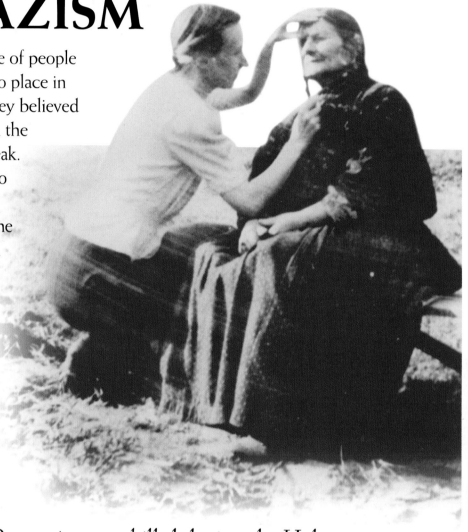

Targeting Romanies

Living a traditional nomadic (moving around with no fixed home) existence, about 30,000 Romanies lived in Greater Germany and 1,000,000 in Eastern Europe, mainly in Romania and the Soviet Union. The Nazis built on a long history of prejudice against Romanies in Europe. They measured their faces, claiming that Romanies, like Jews, were a different race—"life unworthy of life."

About 500,000 Romanies were killed during the Holocaust.

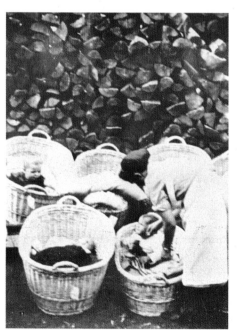

Prejudice against blacks

There were few black people in Germany, and Nazi hatred of them emerged when Germany hosted the Olympic Games in 1936. To avoid shaking the hands of black people who had won medals, such as American Jesse Owens, shown here, Hitler did not shake the hands of any winners. Propaganda Minister Goebbels called successes by black people "a disgrace."

The Germanization of Poles

The Nazis thought the Poles were subhuman and wanted their land. Although the Nazis persecuted the Poles and killed millions of them, they thought some Polish babies and children "looked" German. They kidnapped about 50,000 of them, including these babies in baskets, to be adopted by German parents and "Germanized."

Political opponents

The Nazis would not tolerate opposition, whatever the "race" of the opponents. They banned other political parties and rooted out their members, especially communists because they believed that they conspired with Jews to rule the world. This photograph, taken secretly in 1933, shows one location where political opponents were imprisoned, tortured, and forced into hard labor.

Homosexuals

The Nazis thought that homosexuals were inferior because they would not have children and continue the race. They also believed that homosexual males were not real men. Fearing that homosexuality would spread as a social disease, the Nazis shut down homosexual clubs and bars, such as this one in Berlin in 1933.

People with disabilities

Nazi plans for the perfect race were threatened by the mentally ill and physically disabled, so at least 300,000 people were sterilized in 1934 to stop them from having children. Hereditary health cards like this one were created to track any family history of disability.

Jehovah's Witnesses

Due to their faith, Jehovah's Witnesses do not support a government or carry weapons, so they did not support the Third Reich. By 1935, it was illegal to be a Jehovah's Witness and many were taken to camps. Jehovah's Witness Johannes Steyer painted Hitler as a "saint" to show how most Germans saw him.

WORLD WAR II

THE WORLD WATCHED NAZI GERMANY but did nothing until, in 1938, Hitler made his first moves to dominate Europe. In 1939, when German troops moved into Poland, war was declared. The war between the Allies (Britain, the Soviet Union, the US, and other countries) and the Axis Powers (Germany, Italy, and Japan) was fought over territory, not the Nazis' brutal treament of minority groups.

The invasion of Czechoslovakia

Hitler threatened to invade Czechoslovakia unless Britain supported his plan to take over Sudetenland, an area of German-speaking Czechoslovakia. In September 1938 in Munich, Britain and France agreed that Germany could have Sudetenland. In return, Germany agreed not to occupy more of Europe. On his return, British Prime Minister Neville Chamberlain held up the Munich Agreement and called it "peace in our time." But in March 1939, Germany seized the rest of Czechoslovakia.

German invasion of Poland

On September 1, 1939, German troops advanced into western Poland and Britain declared war on Germany. Within two weeks, Poland was completely occupied and Germany called the territory it captured "The General Government." This train is taking German troops to Poland in late September. The handwriting on the side reads, "We are going to Poland to thrash the Jews."

"The Blitz"

With Britain at war with Germany, there were air raids over London and other cities from August 1940. These raids were nicknamed The Blitz, from the German word *blitzkrieg*, meaning "lightning war." These people are sleeping in one of London's underground stations, which were used as air-raid shelters.

The US enters the war

After the German occupation of France, the US began debating whether to support Britain in the war. Then, on December 7, 1941, Japan, an ally of Germany, attacked Pearl Harbor in Hawaii, US. The next day the US declared war on Japan, and three days later Germany and Italy declared war on the US. This poster encouraged Americans to buy savings bonds to help fund the war.

BUY WAR BONDS

Areas occupied by the Nazis in 1942

- German occupied
- German allies or occupied by German allies
- Neutral
- Allies

The Nazi occupation of Europe

By 1942, Germany had occupied and was controlling more than half of Europe, as well as part of the Soviet Union.

Operation Barbarossa

Germany planned to create a colony within the Soviet Union and invaded in June 1941. Code-named Operation Barbarossa, it involved three million troops and more than 3,000 tanks. The German soldiers and tanks above almost reached Moscow, but suffered such heavy casualties they were eventually forced to surrender.

THE GHETTOS

ALTHOUGH THERE WERE GHETTOS in the Middle Ages to which Jews were restricted, they had all closed down by the beginning of the 19th century. The Nazis revived the idea of the ghettos and used them to confine their victims—mostly Jews, but also Romanies. Conditions in the ghettos were extremely harsh: food and water were scarce, people were crammed together in small spaces, and the constant presence of Nazi troops was very oppressive.

Footbridge in the Łódź ghetto
The sealed ghetto of Łódź Poland, was divided into two parts. Ghetto residents were not allowed to use the streets and could only cross from one part to the other using the footbridge.

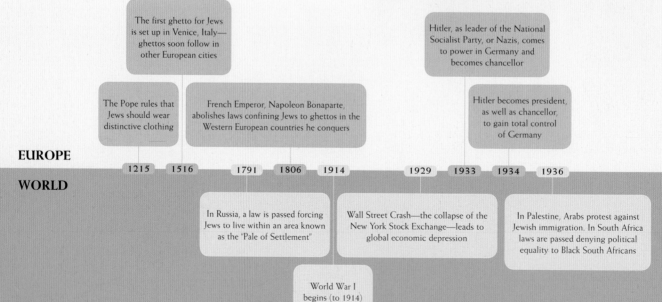

The first ghetto for Jews is set up in Venice, Italy—ghettos soon follow in other European cities

Hitler, as leader of the National Socialist Party, or Nazis, comes to power in Germany and becomes chancellor

The Pope rules that Jews should wear distinctive clothing

French Emperor, Napoleon Bonaparte, abolishes laws confining Jews to ghettos in the Western European countries he conquers

Hitler becomes president, as well as chancellor, to gain total control of Germany

EUROPE

| 1215 | 1516 | 1791 | 1806 | 1914 | 1929 | 1933 | 1934 | 1936 |

WORLD

In Russia, a law is passed forcing Jews to live within an area known as the "Pale of Settlement"

Wall Street Crash—the collapse of the New York Stock Exchange—leads to global economic depression

In Palestine, Arabs protest against Jewish immigration. In South Africa laws are passed denying political equality to Black South Africans

World War I begins (to 1914)

Germany invades Poland. Emmanuel Ringelblum begins his diary in the Warsaw ghetto and sets up the *Oyneg Shabbes* group

Deportation of Jews to death camps from ghettos in Poland, and other areas of German-occupied Europe, begins

Hitler commits suicide in his bunker in Berlin, Germany

Kristallnacht (Night of Broken Glass)—all over Germany, Jews and their property are attacked

Nazis establish a Jewish ghetto in Łódź, Poland

Warsaw ghetto uprising, Poland

The first milk churn of documents hidden by *Oyneg Shabbes* group is discovered in Warsaw

1938	1939	1940	1941	1942	1943	1945	1946	1950

World War II begins (to 1945)

Japan bombs ships in Pearl Harbor, Hawaii

The US drops atomic bombs on Hiroshima and Nagasaki, Japan

In South Africa, laws are passed enforcing a system of racial segregation, called apartheid (to 1994)

First US forces arrive in Europe

GHETTO ORGANIZATIONS

TO CARRY OUT THEIR ORDERS, the Nazis set up *Judenraete*—Jewish councils. A community could elect members of its *Judenrat* only with Nazi approval. The *Judenraete* rightly suspected the Nazis of exploiting them, but did not usually dare disobey orders. Jewish communities expected them to bargain with the Nazis for better conditions, which often made the job of the *Judenraete* a difficult balancing act.

Ghetto money
The Nazis confiscated Jews' money and valuables and, in several ghettos, issued coins and paper currency for use only in that particular ghetto. This ghetto money had no value anywhere else, and Jews called it "Monopoly money." Chaim Rumkowski, leader of the Łódź *Judenrat*, issued currency himself—nicknamed "Rumkies."

Health and welfare
In addition to undertaking the functions that the Nazis demanded, *Judenraete* also took on other roles. They organized families to share rooms, took care of orphans, and also set up clinics, like this one. Despite scant resources, many doctors were courageous and creative. Dr. Vittorio Sacerdoti in Rome invented a disease he called "K Syndrome," which scared the Nazis and spared 45 Jews from deportation.

Ghetto police
The Nazis ordered the *Judenraete* to create ghetto police forces. They were the first Jewish police forces in Europe, carrying out duties dictated by the Nazis and some that the *Judenraete* decided. They also did whatever seemed necessary in the community. Jewish police were recognizable by their uniform and badge.

Sickness and death
Hospitals were managed by *Judenraete* on very scant resources, and doctors faced moral dilemmas about which patients to feed and treat. Handcarts like this were an increasingly common sight in the ghettos and had a dual function—for taking the sick to hospital and the dead to the cemetery.

Work

In order to make the ghettos useful to the Nazis and so reduce the number of Jews deported, *Judenraete* created as many factories and workshops as they could. These Jews in a clothing factory in the Warsaw ghetto were thought fortunate, despite the long hours, because they got extra food rations.

Food rations

Judenraete were responsible for issuing ration cards like this one, entitling the bearer to perhaps 200–300 calories a day or a loaf of bread to last five days. At times there was not even any food available to buy. *Judenraete* also set up communal kitchens, serving people soup or whatever else might be available.

Mind and body

Schools and orphanages were run by the *Judenraete*. If the Nazis closed them down, they operated in secret. Communal kitchens often doubled as informal schools, where teachers told stories and gave out food. This picture, *Story Hour*, painted by Pavel Fantl (1903–45) in Terezin, shows how education helped people survive in the ghettos.

MY SECRET CAMERA

Sensing that the ghetto would not survive, the Łódź *Judenrat* decided to photograph ghetto life so that their story could one day be told. In secret, several workers took photos of what the Nazis did and made them do. One photographer, Henryk Ross, captured everyday life and personal situations. This picture—one of 3,000 he took—shows two boys playing "cops and robbers," one dressed up as a ghetto policeman. Ross survived the Holocaust and found the negatives he had hidden, some of which were in good condition.

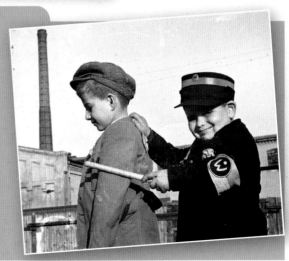

CULTURAL LIFE AND SPIRITUAL RESISTANCE

DESPITE THE HIGH WALLS OF THE GHETTOS and the military strength of the Nazis, many people in the ghettos escaped or fought in their hearts and minds. For most, resistance took the form of clinging to the love of family and friends, holding on to traditions, and strengthening their hope. It was a great tribute to the human spirit that, even though the Nazis tried to dehumanize them, the Jews went to great lengths to preserve their humanity.

Jewish youth movements
Youth groups became even more important after the Nazis closed the schools. They offered young people education or training, involved them in welfare work, and gave them inspiration and hope for the future. Here, members of the Front of the Wilderness Generation in Lodz are enjoying themselves in a circle dance.

Children in the ghettos
Many children's parents died from starvation or disease, or were deported. In Warsaw, Janusz Korczak ran a large orphanage. When the Nazis deported the children to a death camp, he went with them so that they would not be alone. This event is portrayed in this sculpture in the Warsaw Jewish cemetery.

Starving and studying
In Warsaw, ghetto doctors decided that some good should come from the starvation that everyone experienced. They studied the effects of malnutrition on the mind and body, and their very useful research was published after the Holocaust. Here, medical staff, who themselves are starving, are trying to treat a starving patient in hospital.

Crying and laughing

Many people found they could forget their suffering for a while by listening to or performing music, like those in this ghetto orchestra. Jews needed to express their sadness, but also often made jokes about the conditions in the ghetto. Several ghettos had thriving Jewish theaters, which meant a lot to both the actors and the audience. Crying and laughing together was an important way for those in the ghettos to feel that they were still human, whatever their situation.

More than 6,000 drawings and paintings were hidden in the Terezin ghetto during the Holocaust.

"The Führer builds the Jews a Town"

Terezin, which the Nazis called Theresienstadt, was a so-called "model ghetto" in Czechoslovakia. People could get art materials and created many drawings and paintings, like this one by a child, expressing memories of a happier life. But a Nazi propaganda film hugely exaggerated the education and cultural activities that went on and pretended it was a town that Hitler built specially for the Jews.

Praying and praising

Jewish worship continued in the ghettos and was even more intense during the Holocaust, despite (or perhaps because of) the fact that the Nazis forbade it. Many, like this group studying Jewish texts in the Krakow ghetto, made huge sacrifices to practice their religion, running the risk of being caught.

Adam Czerniakow, Warsaw

As head of the Warsaw *Judenrat*, Czerniakow received the announcement, in July 1942, that the Nazis intended to deport 6,000 Jews each day until none remained. Czerniakow managed to get exemptions for a few, including the girl in this photo, but the Nazis would not spare the children in the Korczak orphanage. The next day, as an act of protest, Czerniakow took his own life.

Yakob Gens, Vilna

The Nazis abolished the Vilna *Judenrat* and put Gens, former head of the ghetto police, in charge. When they demanded victims, he chose the elderly, believing that a productive ghetto would survive. His goal was to ensure that at least some would live, and he explained that if he did not hand over a thousand Jews, the Nazis would take 10 thousand. He once said, "May the aged among the Jews forgive us. They were a sacrifice for our Jews and our future."

Chaim Rumkowski, Łódź

Rumkowski—shown here with the Nazi head of the ghetto administration—was nicknamed "King Chaim." He believed that the way to protect most Jews was to give the Nazis whatever they asked for. When deportation calls came, he urged parents to surrender their children.

LIQUIDATION OF THE GHETTOS

EVEN AS THE GHETTOS WERE EMPTIED, it was not always clear to their inhabitants what lay ahead. Jews had varying fantasies and fears about their destinations. Some knew about the death camps and did not resist deportation. Some tried to escape. Others did not know or did not want to know.

Filling and emptying
The gross overcrowding in this room in Poland was typical of ghettos everywhere. Often several families had to share a single room, and personal family conversations or privacy between a husband and wife were impossible. People burned their furniture for cooking and heating, and had to sleep on the floor—sometimes in shifts.

Saying goodbye
The liquidation of the ghettos separated many families. This mother is being parted from her son. Sometimes children were deported because they were less useful to the Nazis. Parents being deported sometimes hid their children or entrusted them to anyone who could take them.

A farewell letter
Zipporah Berman sent this tender and loving note to her sister, who was already living in the Land of Israel, knowing that she might never see her again. She wrote in Hebrew, which she learned because she also hoped to go and live in the Jewish homeland.

A final wave
From some ghettos, deportations were by train. Here, though, Jews are crowded onto open trucks, meaning the journey may only have been a few hours long. We might wonder who these women are waving to as they are carted off, and whether they know where they are being taken and what will happen to them.

LARGEST GHETTOS	
Warsaw, Poland	400,000–500,000
Łódź, Poland	205,000
Lvov, Ukraine	110,000
Minsk, Belorussia	100,000
Terezin, Czechoslovakia	90,000
Budapest, Hungary	70,000
Chernovtsy, Romania	50,000
Białystok, Poland	35,000–50,000
Riga, Latvia	43,000
Vilna, Lithuania	41,000
Kovno, Lithuania	40,000
Lublin, Poland	34,000

Population figures of the largest ghettos
Within months these large populations of Jews were reduced to just a few thousand, as the Nazis carried out mass deportations.

THE WARSAW GHETTO UPRISING

THE WARSAW GHETTO UPRISING was one of the most remarkable events of the Holocaust. The Jewish resistance fighters were hugely outnumbered by the Nazis, yet they succeeded in denting Nazi capability and confidence. They inspired the breakout from the Treblinka death camp and an uprising in the rest of Warsaw.

Map Key

- ▉ 1943 ghetto at the time of the uprising
- ▢ 1940 ghetto
- — Boundary of the ghetto on July 22, 1942 when the deportations began
- ● Entrance to the ghetto in 1940
- ● Entrance to the ghetto in 1942
- ▢ SS Office for valuables taken from Jews
- ▲ Bunkers and fighting points

The largest ghetto
When the Nazis created the Warsaw ghetto in October 1940, some 350,000 Jews lived in the city—about 30 percent of the population. The ghetto was 20 times more densely populated than the rest of Warsaw and, as this map shows, the Nazis reduced the space even more.

Walls all around
In November 1940, the Nazis enclosed the ghetto by making the Jews build a 10-ft (3-m) high wall around it. They aimed to make it impossible for Jews to reach other parts of Warsaw. Despite this, the Jewish Military Union (ZZW) organized the smuggling of food and weapons.

From Warsaw to…?
In July 1942, the Nazis announced that they would resettle 6,000 Jews per day "in the East." This was alarming, but the Jews did not know exactly what it meant. By September, 300,000 had been transported from this station to a death camp, where most were killed immediately. About 55,000 people were left in the ghetto.

During the Warsaw ghetto uprising, the Germans had 135 machine guns to the Jews' two machine guns, and 1,358 rifles to the Jews' 15 rifles.

The ghetto fights back
In January 1943, during a deportation, members of the Jewish Fighting Organization (ZOB) fired on German troops. The troops retreated after a few days. Although the victory was temporary, it encouraged the fighters. This memorial in Warsaw commemorates their determination.

The ghetto rises in revolt
On April 19, 1943, German troops and police entered the ghetto to deport anyone still there. It was the eve of Passover, the Jewish festival of freedom—and that theme was in the hearts of the 750 Jewish fighters in the ghetto, who were determined to fight to the finish. General Jürgen Stroop, the head of the police, ordered his troops to set the ghetto on fire.

The struggle continues
The fire raged and the fighters were vastly outnumbered by Nazis. Even knowing that they had no chance, they still refused to surrender. Many took to bunkers in the cellars, and some moved from building to building through the sewers. Others were captured amid the rubble.

The revolt is crushed
Having ordered the sewers to be flooded, Stroop finally crushed the revolt on May 16, 1943. Of the 55,000 Jews captured, about 7,000 were shot and the rest deported to death camps. In his report Stroop wrote, "The ghetto is no more." The fighters had held out for three weeks—three weeks longer than Stroop thought his forces would need to overpower them.

THE RINGELBLUM ARCHIVE

In many ghettos, Jews felt the need to record their experiences so that the world would know—either then or later—what was happening. The most wide-ranging collection was in Warsaw. The Ringelblum Archive, named after the historian who started the research, is a major source of information about Nazi activities, conditions in the ghettos, and how Jews responded.

Emmanuel Ringelblum
Ringelblum started a diary in 1939, subsequently using it to record and reflect on ghetto life. He would write for hours in the library (left, in photo), which still stands, though the Great Synagogue next to it was destroyed by the Nazis. When the deportations began, he wanted to reflect a wider range of ghetto experiences and ideas so he urged others to join in his research and creativity.

"Sabbath delight"
The Ringelblum group met in the library on Saturday afternoons and called themselves *Oyneg Shabbes*, meaning "Sabbath delight." They wrote and drew on any scraps of paper they could get. They also collected writings and drawings by children and adults, and examples of community events like the concert advertised in this poster. Ringelblum was extremely proud of the way the group worked together toward a common goal.

"Between life and death"
The *Oyneg Shabbes* group thought that if the free world knew the truth about the ghettos, it might strengthen the fight against Nazism. Seeing it as an act of resistance, they contributed all kinds of material to the archive. Gela Seksztajn, who donated this self-portrait, described herself as "at the boundary between life and death" and urged Jews to do everything to stop the tragedy from being repeated.

The Ringelblum Archive contains approximately 25,000 pages of testimony, artworks, literature, and correspondence.

Churns and cans

When it became clear that most Warsaw Jews would be killed, the *Oyneg Shabbes* group decided to leave their work as a witness to their lives. They buried their material in milk churns and metal boxes in three different places. The last was buried on the eve of the ghetto uprising.

Unearthing a find

The Nazis discovered the *Oyneg Shabbes* leaders and shot them. The only leader to survive the Holocaust was Hersz Wasser, Ringelblum's assistant. He remembered where some of the churns and cans were buried and in 1946 helped dig them out (pictured right). A second cache was unearthed in 1950, but the third was never discovered.

Sifting and sorting

The library where the *Oyneg Shabbes* group used to meet is now the site of the Jewish Historical Institute. Here, archivists from the Institute are sorting through some of the material found in the rusty churns soon after it was discovered. The material had been buried quickly and was in poor condition when it was dug up.

Scream the truth

Dawid Graber was 19 when he helped to bury the first cache in August 1942. It contained this page, his last will and testament. It sustained water damage, but under a microscope, the writing is clear: "I would love to see the moment when the great treasure will be dug up and scream the truth at the world… May the treasure fall into good hands, may it last into better times, may it alarm and alert the world."

THE MURDER OF THE VICTIMS

THE DELIBERATE KILLING of people who the Nazis believed had no right to live became known as the Holocaust. Various methods were used to make these murders ever more systematic and efficient. Between 1933 and 1945, more than 10 million men, women, and children were murdered—about six million of these were Jews and about half a million were Romanies.

Cattle cars
The majority of people deported to labor and death camps were transported in cattle wagons, such as this one. Inside, conditions were desperately cramped and the air was stifling. Many died on the way.

Nazi Party, led by Adolf Hitler, comes to power in Germany. First German concentration camp for political prisoners set up at Dachau, Germany

Concentration camp set up at Sachsenhausen in Germany

Concentration camps set up at Flossenbürg in Germany and Mauthausen in Austria

Hitler becomes president, gaining total control of Germany

Concentration camp set up at Buchenwald, Germany

Concentration camp set up at Ravensbrück, Germany. The SS becomes a central department of the Nazi government

EUROPE

1914 1917   1920 1922 1933 1934   1936 1937   1938 1939

WORLD

World War I begins (to 1918)

British Mandate (administration) of Palestine begins (to 1948)

In Palestine, Arabs protest against Jewish immigration

World War II begins (to 1945)

The Russian Revolution sees the czar abdicate and the Bolsheviks (communists) come to power

Russia becomes the Union of Soviet Socialist Republics (USSR)

Camps set up at Chelmno, Majdanek, and Auschwitz-Birkenau in occupied Poland, and at Terezin (Theresienstadt), now in the Czech Republic. Massacre of 33,771 Jews at Babi Yar, Ukraine

Camp at Bergen-Belsen, in Germany, becomes a concentration camp

Nuremberg war crimes trials of Nazi leaders begin in Germany

Nazi plan to deport Europe's Jews to Madagascar, off the coast of Africa, abandoned. Camps set up at Auschwitz in Poland

At Wannsee Conference, Berlin, Nazis commit to the "Final Solution." Camps set up at Belzec, Treblinka, and Sobibor in Poland. *Einsatzgruppen* (Nazi killing squads) enter Soviet Union

Germany invades and occupies Hungary. Mass deportation of Hungarian Jews to Auschwitz. Romania withdraws from the war

1940 **1941** **1942** **1943** **1944** **1945** **1948**

Japan bombs American ships in Pearl Harbor, Hawaii

US drops atomic bombs on Hiroshima and Nagasaki, Japan

First US forces arrive in Europe

Jewish State of Israel declared. Arab-Israeli War begins (to 1949)

CONCENTRATION CAMPS IN GERMANY

Camp locations in Germany 1933–45

- ☐ Large camp
- ○ City
- ◾ Smaller camp
- — Bordering country

German camps

Most concentration camps in Germany were labor camps, but some were collection points where people were held before being moved to another camp. Others were temporary holding places for the dying. By 1939, hundreds of small camps had been merged into seven large camps, including Mauthausen in annexed Austria.

DENMARK

NETHERLANDS

Ravensbrück

Bergen-Belsen

Sachsenhausen Berlin

BELGIUM

Buchenwald

Flossenbürg

PROTECTORATE OF BOHEMIA AND MORAVIA

FRANCE

Nuremberg

SLOVAKIA

Dachau

Mauthausen

0 km   100   200   300

0 miles   100   200

Munich

SWITZERLAND

HUNGARY

ITALY

CROATIA

CONCENTRATION CAMPS

were first set up in 1933. Initially, their purpose was to hold "undesirables" and political opponents of the Nazis. However, some families with children were also detained in concentration camps. Although the main purpose of the camps was not to kill people, many died because their health was neglected or they were treated brutally. In all the camps, the detainees were dehumanized and treated as mere objects.

CAMP	OPERATED	PRISONERS	DEATHS
Bergen-Belsen	1943–45	unknown	70,000
Buchenwald	1937–45	250,000	56,000
Dachau	1933–45	200,000	30,000
Flossenbürg	1938–45	>100,000	30,000
Mauthausen	1938–45	195,000	>95,000
Ravensbrück	1939–45	150,000	>90,000
Sachsenhausen	1936–45	>200,000	100,000

OCCUPIED EASTERN TERRITORY

GENERAL GOVERNMENT (OCCUPIED POLAND)

Forced labor

Prisoners worked long hours at least six days a week, often in difficult, dirty, or dangerous conditions. As well as construction sites and quarries, there were workshops and factories that made items for the German government. In 1938, the SS began using forced camp labor for profit.

A poor diet

There was never enough food for the detainees. The food was always the same, so people did not get a balanced diet and some starved to death. These women at Mauthausen are lining up for soup, usually made with potatoes and cabbage. The other main food was bread.

Medical experiments

Some camps used detainees to test new products and procedures. For example, experiments to investigate how much pain people could endure in a compression chamber occurred at Dachau in 1942. The findings would assist the German Air Force, but the research was painful for the participants. This Romany detainee is in agony, after being forced to drink saltwater to test whether it is drinkable.

Living conditions

People were made to live in very unpleasant and unhealthy conditions. These prisoners at Buchenwald are crammed together in shared bunks, which made sleep difficult. The camps were also filthy. Most of the time there was no hot water for washing, and sometimes there was no water at all. During the summer the camps were stiflingly hot, and in the winter they were bitterly cold.

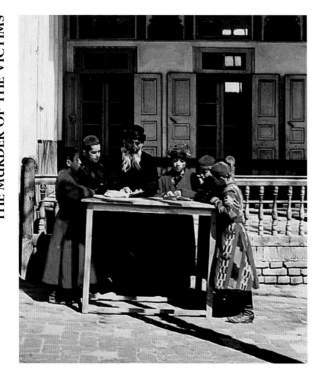

Jewish life before the Russian Revolution
For centuries, Jewish life in Russia revolved around the Jewish traditions of prayer, study, and charitable deeds. In the shtetl, the synagogue was the heart of the Jewish community, and education focused on discussing the meaning of the traditional texts, like these boys studying the Torah with their teacher.

THE JEWS OF THE SOVIET UNION

JEWS HAD LIVED IN RUSSIAN LANDS for about 1,500 years, but from the end of the 19th century, anti-Semitism forced many to immigrate to the West or to Palestine. Many who stayed became involved in groups fighting for a more equal society, but even those groups were anti-Semitic. So, in 1897, Jews created their own movement, called the Bund. This revived Jewish self-confidence and developed a modern Jewish culture, still active when Russia became the Soviet Union after the revolution of 1917.

Jews under the rule of communism
In the revolution of 1917, the Russian Empire was overthrown and the communists eventually created the Union of Soviet Socialist Republics (USSR). Many idealistic Jews believed that it would bring a better world, but anti-Semitism continued. There was no place for Jews in the new system unless they gave up their way of life. In this photo, Jews are protesting about the use of Jewish headstones for construction projects.

Firing squad
In June 1941, mobile killing units, called *Einsatzgruppen*, entered the Soviet Union on instructions from Nazi leader Heydrich. They were to kill Jews, communists, and other Nazi enemies. The people shot by this firing squad, and most victims, were Jews. Local people were aware of these shootings, which usually happened in broad daylight.

Areas of German and Soviet occupation

- German annexation of Austria, March 1938
- German annexation from Czechoslovakia, November 1938–March 1939
- German annexation of Memel, Danzig, and from Poland, 1939
- Hungarian annexation from Czechoslovakia, 1938–39
- Hungarian annexation from Romania, 1940
- Soviet annexation from Poland, September 1939
- Soviet annexation from Romania, 1940
- Soviet annexation of Baltic countries, 1940
- Lithuanian annexation from Poland, September 1939
- — Boundary between German and Soviet spheres of influence

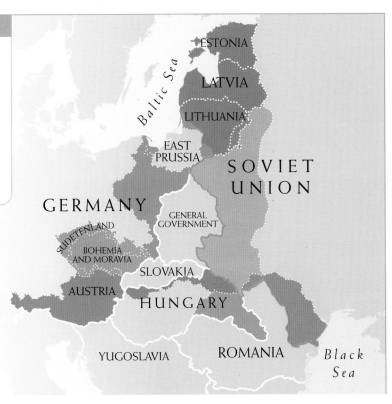

Nazi-Soviet nonaggression pact

As Germany prepared to invade Poland in 1939, it signed a nonaggression pact with the USSR—an agreement not to invade or attack each other. As this map shows, they shared the areas of Eastern Europe between them. This split Poland in two. General Government was the name for the area of Poland not incorporated into the Third Reich.

0 km	200	400	600	800	1,000

0 miles	200	400	600

At Babi Yar, more than 33,000 Jews were killed in just two days.

Babi Yar uncovered

In September 1941, Jews in Kiev, Ukraine, were herded to the Babi Yar ravine. Ukrainian police forced them to undress and walk to its edge. When German troops shot them, they fell into the abyss. The Germans pushed the wall of the ravine over, burying the dead and the living. Despite attempts to destroy the evidence, Soviet investigators discovered the bodies in 1943.

Massacre at Babi Yar

The Babi Yar massacre was the most intensive Holocaust killing. Nazis reported killing 33,771 Jews in two days, and later killed more Jews, Romanies, Soviet prisoners of war, and Ukrainian nationalists. The Soviet estimate is 100,000. Police grabbed children like these and flung them into the ravine.

"They took my mother and shot her too ... and then my grandmother, my father's mother, she was eighty years old and she had two children in her arms, and then there was my father's sister. She also had children in her arms and she was shot on the spot with the babies in her arms..."

Rivka Yosselevscka, who survived the Einsatzgruppen *in Zagrodski in 1942, giving evidence at a war crimes tribunal court*

A mother attempts to shield the child in her arms, as she is about to be shot by the *Einsatzgruppen*

THE JEWS OF ROMANIA

JEWISH ORIGINS IN ROMANIA date back to the 2nd century CE. In later centuries, Jews migrated into Romania from other parts of Europe, especially those Jews expelled from Spain. Before the Holocaust, Romania had the third largest Jewish community in Eastern Europe, and life was fairly untroubled. However, severe anti-Semitic activity after World War I prompted many Jews to leave Romania and prepare for a new life in Palestine.

Romania and surrounding regions, 1941
The territory of Romania changed during the Holocaust, as regions were occupied by Hungary (northern Transylvania) and Bulgaria (southern Dobrudja). Romania occupied the Transnistria area of Ukraine in the Soviet Union, and transported Jews and Romanies there.

In Odessa and the surrounding area 40,000 Jews were killed between October 23–25, 1942.

Iron Guard
The Legionnaires began in Romania in 1927 as an ultranationalistic, anti-Semitic movement, which lasted into the 1940s. Officially called the Legion of the Archangel Michael, its patron saint is shown here. In 1930, the Iron Guard was formed as a paramilitary branch of the Legion. The Iron Guard massacred Jews when Romania lost land to the Soviet Union.

Antonescu's government
In 1940, Romania became a satellite of Nazi Germany. Inspired by the Nuremberg laws, the government of General Ion Antonescu, shown here with Hitler, made 80 harsh anti-Jewish laws and statements. It also massacred 7,000 Romanies, deporting and starving thousands of others, and killed up to 380,000 Jews—the greatest number outside Germany.

From Iasi to Calarasi

The Iasi massacre in June 1941 was the most dreadful in Romania. With rumors of the Soviets landing, an estimated 14,000 Jews were shot. The 4,330 survivors were taken in sealed cargo trains to camps at Calarasi and other places. About 2,500 died from suffocation, thirst, or starvation. When trains were stopped to remove the dead, more Jews were killed by local people.

Terror in Bucharest

For three days in January 1941, the Iron Guard and Bucharest hooligans terrorized Jews in the streets and in their homes. They arrested thousands, seizing and vandalizing Jewish property and belongings. Many synagogues were desecrated and two, including this one, were set alight. Many Jews were killed, and their bodies hung up on hooks.

The Odessa massacre

Odessa in Transnistria was part of the Ukraine. When the Germans occupied the area in late 1941, Romanians and Germans began exterminating the Jewish population of 300,000. Some were hanged in the street, some shot, and some burned alive.

Bessarabia and Bukovina

Half of the 320,000 Jews in Bessarabia and Bukovina were murdered in 1941. More than 123,000 were deported in forced marches, and on rafts like this, to death camps in Transnistria. The Germans shot some and sent the rest back. Many drowned, others died on the way, or in camps set up in Bukovina and Bessarabia.

A chance to leave

In December 1942, Romania allowed the Transnistria Jews to go as illegal immigrants to Palestine. In 1944, when Romania changed sides in the war, 13 boats had left. Two of them, including the *Struma*, shown here with 769 passengers on board, tragically sank during the voyage.

THE FINAL SOLUTION

THE NAZIS CALLED THEIR PLAN to exterminate Europe's Jews the "Final Solution." They saw the Jews as a problem that had to be solved, and the removal or, preferably, destruction of all Jews was the solution they wanted. Although they had already murdered more than a million Jews, the Nazis still thought of other ways to kill them more quickly and efficiently.

The Madagascar Plan
In 1940, the Nazis had the idea of taking over France and moving large groups of Jews to the French colony of Madagascar, off Africa. But the plan required the British navy to transport the Jews and, because Britain had not been defeated, the idea was scrapped.

AKTION REINHARD

The plan to exterminate Polish Jews was code-named *Aktion Reinhard*—named after Reinhard Heydrich, one of the leading planners of the "Final Solution." In order to carry out the plan, in 1942 extermination, or death, camps were built in Poland at Belzec, Sobibor, and Treblinka. This graph shows the numbers of victims murdered in each of the six main camps in Poland. Two million Jews were exterminated through *Aktion Reinhard*.

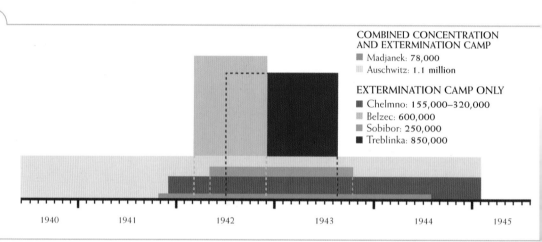

COMBINED CONCENTRATION AND EXTERMINATION CAMP
■ Madjanek: 78,000
□ Auschwitz: 1.1 million

EXTERMINATION CAMP ONLY
■ Chelmno: 155,000–320,000
■ Belzec: 600,000
■ Sobibor: 250,000
■ Treblinka: 850,000

| 1940 | 1941 | 1942 | 1943 | 1944 | 1945 |

At the Wannsee Conference, Estonia was marked as being Jew-free. Every one of the country's 1,000 Jews had been murdered.

The Wannsee Conference
In January 1942, fourteen high-ranking Nazis met in this big house in Wannsee, a suburb of Berlin. Heydrich chaired the meeting that planned the "Final Solution," the program to deport all Jews east, where the SS would kill them. The meeting was top secret but notes were found in 1947.

Europe 1942

■ German occupied		□ Neutral	
□ German ally		■ Allies	

Jews marked out for death

One of the papers presented at the Wannsee Conference included a list of the numbers of Jews living in various parts of Europe in January 1942—those areas that the Germans intended to conquer, and those already under German control. The numbers of Jews that the Germans planned to exterminate are shown here by country.

NORWAY 1,300
SWEDEN 8,000
FINLAND 2,300
ESTONIA "Free of Jews"
SOVIET UNION 5,000,000 (including White Russia and Ukraine)
LATVIA 3,500
IRELAND 4,000
GREAT BRITAIN 330,000
DENMARK 5,600
LITHUANIA 34,000
WHITE RUSSIA 445,484
BIALYSTOK DISTRICT 400,000
NETHERLANDS 160,800
GREATER GERMANY 131,800
EASTERN TERRITORIES 420,000
GENERAL GOVERNMENT 2,284,000
UKRAINE 2,994,684
BELGIUM 43,000
PROTECTORATE OF BOHEMIA AND MORAVIA 74,200
OCCUPIED FRANCE 165,000
SLOVAKIA 88,000
SWITZERLAND 18,000
AUSTRIA 43,700
HUNGARY 742,800
VICHY FRANCE 700,000 (including French North Africa)
CROATIA 40,000
SERBIA 10,000
ROMANIA 342,000
PORTUGAL 3,000
SPAIN 6,000
ITALY 58,000
MONTENEGRO
BULGARIA 48,000
EUROPEAN TURKEY 55,000
ALBANIA 200
TURKEY
GREECE 69,000
CYPRUS

0 km 500 1,000 1,500
0 miles 500 1,000

DEPT	SS ROLES AND RESPONSIBILITIES
I	**Human Resources** Supervising Nazi agents and training collaborators
II	**Organization, administration, and law** Banishing "Enemies of the State" and Jews, and seizing their possessions; construction of gas vans
II	**Domestic news service** Collecting and interpreting reports about the effects policies were having on the population; also judging whether people selected for a role were politically suitable
IV	**Gestapo** Persecuting (harassing) real or supposed opponents; included the section IV B4, in which Eichmann planned "The final solution to the Jewish problem" and deportation to death camps
V	**Criminal police** Prosecuting (taking legal action against) nonpolitical crimes, abusing gypsies and disabled people
VI	**Foreign news service** Espionage (spying) and counterespionage abroad
VII	**Research and assessment** Collecting and assessing the value of seized books and other materials

Central SS administration

The SS, short for *Schutzstaffel*, which means "protective squadron," began as Hitler's bodyguard. Under Heinrich Himmler, it grew into a force of 600,000 men, separate from the army. In 1939, the SS became a central department and Heydrich its chief. The main divisions are shown on this chart from 1940.

Nazi chain of command

The Nazi organization was extremely tightly structured, with clear lines of command between members. Adolf Eichmann ran Gestapo Department IV B4 and, at his trial in 1961, he drew this chart of the organization, which was submitted in evidence.

The pile of shoes of the victims in block 4, Auschwitz 1, photographed in 1995 as an exhibit for the museum we discussed the ways and means of effecting the extermination. This could only be done by gassing, since it would have been absolutely impossible to dispose by shooting of the large numbers of people that were expected, and it would have placed too heavy a burden on the SS men who had to carry it out, especially because of the women and children among the victims."

Rudolf Hoess, on his meeting with Himmler in summer 1941

LABOR CAMPS

CAMPS WERE ORIGINALLY INTENDED to imprison the people that the Nazis most despised. But when World War II began, the purpose of the camps changed to forced labor and outright murder. By 1942, extermination through work was official policy, and prisoners in all the concentration camps were—quite literally—worked to death.

Work brings freedom
A German sign, such as the one below, hung over the gates of five labor camps. The Nazis may have used "Work Brings Freedom" seriously or as a cruel joke, but people in labor camps were definitely not free. If the Nazis thought a person was unfit and could not work they would be killed, and no matter how hard a person worked, they would never be freed.

ARBEIT MACHT FREI

A complex of camps
Many of the larger labor camps also had smaller subcamps. This map shows the many subcamps of Auschwitz in occupied Poland. Auschwitz and Majdanek were labor and extermination camps where inmates died from illness, injury, exhaustion, or gassing.

WARTHEGAU

GREATER GERMANY

UPPER SILESIA

LOWER SILESIA

GENERAL GOVERNMENT

Hubertushütte
Eintrachthütte Bismarckhütte
Laurahütte
Blechhammer Lagischa
Neustadt Hindenburg Kattowitz
Gleiwitz Sosnowitz & Fürstengrube
(I,II,III&IV) Althammer Neu Dachs
Günthergrube Chelmek Kunzendorf
Charlottegrube Kobior Janinagrube
Babitz Bobrek
Lichtewerden Altdorf Auschwitz II
Freudenthal Tschechowitz Auschwitz III
Plawy Auschwitz I
Golleschau Raisko
Jawischowitz
Harmense
Budy

LOWER SILESIA

SUDETENLAND

PROTECTORATE OF BOHEMIA AND MORAVIA

SLOVAKIA

0 km	25	50	75	100
0 miles		25		50

The growth of camps
Nazi labor camps held prisoners from almost every country in Europe. From 1939, there was a huge rise in the number of camps and prisoners. The SS claimed there were more than 700,000 prisoners in camps by 1945. This aerial view shows the scale and organization of the camp at Majdanek in Poland.

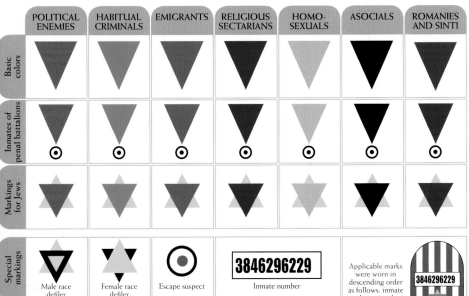

Stolen property

Prisoners at labor camps had all their belongings taken away. Money and valuables, sentimental items such as photographs, and practical items such as eyeglasses were confiscated. Valuables were sold to make money for Germany, such as these wedding rings taken from women at Buchenwald in Germany.

Uniforms

In most labor camps, uniforms were standard. Men wore a jacket such as this, with pants and a cap. Women had a dress and headscarf of the same material. There was no underwear. On their feet prisoners wore wooden clogs, which caused blisters. Uniform had to be worn all the time, even at night.

	POLITICAL ENEMIES	HABITUAL CRIMINALS	EMIGRANTS	RELIGIOUS SECTARIANS	HOMO-SEXUALS	ASOCIALS	ROMANIES AND SINTI
Basic colors	▼	▼	▼	▼	▼	▼	▼
Inmates of penal battalions	⊙	⊙	⊙	⊙	⊙	⊙	⊙
Markings for Jews	✡	✡	✡	✡	✡	✡	✡

Special markings				
▽ Male race defiler	▼ Female race defiler	⊙ Escape suspect	**3846296229** Inmate number	Applicable marks were worn in descending order as follows: inmate number, triangle or star, member of penal battalion, escape suspect
P Pole	T *Tscheche*, German for Czech	△ Member of Armed Forces	⬭ Special inmate: brown arm band	

Numbers and badges

Each prisoner had a number, which was sewn onto their uniform. Guards and other officials called prisoners by their numbers, instead of their names. Other cloth badges, shown here, were used to identify where a prisoner came from and why the Nazis selected them for the camp. An inmate would usually have at least two symbols, but could have more than six.

Types of work

Prisoners carried out different tasks in labor camps. Most of the work involved hard labor, such as clearing this site in Dachau. Some people worked in factories, producing items to support the German economy or ammunition to support Germany in the war.

ROUNDING UP THE VICTIMS

THE NAZIS' COLLECTION of their victims for labor or extermination required excellent organization and a complex system of transportation. Victims were rounded up, often by force, and told to report to a certain place, bringing only a small amount of food and some clothing. They did not know where they were going or what would happen to them.

Nazi camps
☐ Labor camps
☐ Transit camps
☐ Extermination camps

NORWAY

SWEDEN

FINLAND

IRELAND

UNITED KINGDOM

DENMARK

NETHERLANDS

Bredtveit (1942)
Berg (1942)☐ ☐Grini

Klooga☐   ☐Valvara
                              ☐Lagedi

SOVIET UNION

☐ Kaiserwald

OCCUPIED EASTERN TERRITORY

Horserød

Skarzysko-Kamienna

Westerbork
Bergen-Belsen
Mechelen
Breendonk
Compiègne
Drancy
Pithiviers
Vittel

Neuengamme
Vught
Ravensbrück
Sachsenhausen
Dora-Mittelbau
Buchenwald
Fünfbrunnen
Flossenbürg
Natzweiler-Struthof
Schirmeck-Vorbruck

Stutthof

Poniatowa
                      ☐Koldichevo
Chelmno   Treblinka
GREATER   Majdanek
GERMANY   Sobibor
Gross-Rosen   Trawniki
                      Belzec
PROTECTORATE   Janowska
OF BOHEMIA
AND MORAVIA   Budzyn
Auschwitz   Starachowice
Mauthausen   Plaszow

GENERAL GOVERNMENT

FRANCE

SWITZERLAND

Dachau
Bolzano

SLOVAKIA

HUNGARY

Gurs
Rivesaltes

Fossoli di Carpi

San Sabba

Sajmiste

ROMANIA

Schabatz
SERBIA
Nisch

BULGARIA

PORTUGAL

SPAIN

ITALY

CROATIA

MONTENEGRO

ALBANIA

Salonika

TURKEY

GREECE

0 km   250   500   750
0 miles   250   500

Camps in Europe

The Nazis rounded up victims by first taking them to a transit camp. These camps were temporary and people were not usually forced into hard labor. At this stage, they had no idea that conditions where they were heading would be much harsher. The map above shows some of the Nazi camps in occupied Europe. Although there are three types of camps, some had more than one function.

False sense of security

Westerbork transit camp was set up after Germany occupied the Netherlands in 1942. Jews deported to Westerbork were destined for one of five concentration or extermination camps. They were lulled into a false sense of security because of the shops and other features of normal life there. Jews were even allowed some of their religious customs, such as lighting candles for Hanukkah, shown here.

Drancy transit camp

Although there were no ghettos in Western Europe, the camp at Drancy, near Paris, was like a ghetto. The buildings were like prisons, and there was severe overcrowding. Food was in short supply and served communally. Most Jews were taken from Drancy to Auschwitz and murdered on arrival.

The ghetto-camp of Terezin

In 1941, the Nazis turned the prison in Terezin into a cross between a ghetto and a camp and renamed it Theresienstadt. When the Red Cross asked to inspect a camp, Terezin became a showcase, as shown by these Jews sitting in a fake café. For these visits, the Nazis also arranged concerts, soccer or tennis games, and other activities to make it seem a happy, healthy place.

About 15,000 children passed through the Terezin ghetto between 1941 and 1944. Only about 100 of them survived the Holocaust.

The Red Cross comes to check

The conditions were better in Terezin than in concentration camps, but not as good as the Nazis pretended. This 12-year-old girl's painting shows how deceitful the Nazis were. The Red Cross inspectors' vehicles are arriving in Terezin—and the Nazis are quickly ordering everything to be brightened up.

DEATH CAMPS

THE NAZIS BUILT SIX CAMPS for the purpose of carrying out mass murder. All the camps were based in Poland at Auschwitz, Belzec, Chelmno, Majdanek, Sobibor, and Treblinka. Auschwitz and Majdanek also functioned as labour camps. Most people killed in the death camps were Jewish, but there were large numbers from other groups, especially Polish people in Majdanek and Romanies in Belzec and Auschwitz-Birkenau.

On arrival
People arriving at the death camps were faced with harsh conditions and brutal treatment, yet many had no real idea of what would happen. These Romany families at Belzec death camp are waiting for instructions from their captors. They will be stripped of everything – their clothes, their belongings, their names, and their lives.

Transport to the camps
Most people arrived at the camps by train. Those who survived the journey were often weak and sick. Artist and Holocaust survivor David Olère painted *Arrival of a Convoy* in which prisoners drag a heavy cart of corpses to be buried or burned. More prisoners are arriving on the train behind.

Security and control
Death camps were surrounded by walls or electrified fences, with high watchtowers, like this one at Sobibor. The inmates were under the constant watch of the guards, who would often beat, torture, or kill them for no reason.

Disguise and deception
Most camps were built in isolated areas. The Nazis kept their true purpose hidden to prevent panic or anger among the victims. Those sent to gas chambers were told they were showers. Deception was especially strong at Treblinka, as this plan shows, with its station sign, fake ticket office, zoo, and garden.

Killings by shooting
Guards often shot prisoners for minor offences, such as disobeying an order or stealing food. If someone escaped, some of the inmates still in the camp were killed as a punishment and to discourage others from attempting to escape. This woman, in light clothing, has been taken into the snow at Belzec to be shot.

Killing in gas vans
These people in Chelmno death camp are about to enter one of the gas vans that were permanently stationed there from 1941. Chelmno was the first of the camps to use poison gas as a means of taking life. Among the many victims killed there were the 250,000 Jews from the Łódź ghetto.

More than 66,500 Warsaw Jews were killed at Treblinka in its first month.

Gas chambers
Gas vans were replaced by larger, brick gas chambers, which also used carbon monoxide. Later, Zyklon B was developed to kill inmates, and it came packaged in tins such as these. Pellets were dropped through the ceiling of the gas chamber. Zyklon B was safe for the guards to handle, but death was slow and agonizing.

Disposing of the dead
Some of the inmates were forced to remove dead bodies from the gas chambers. At first, corpses were buried, but Nazi leaders felt that cremation – burning the bodies – was more efficient and more hygienic. Crematoria were built, resembling hot "ovens" large enough to take more than one body. Here billowing smoke is seen rising from the crematoria in Majdanek.

VOICES
LIFE IN THE DEATH CAMPS

The horror of the death camps is hard to understand for most people today. For those who survived, the extreme cold, the disease, the abuse, the starvation, the loss of loved ones, and the constant fear of being sent to the gas chamber remain all too clear in their minds.

"I DIDN'T KNOW *what was happening but I knew it was something terrible happening and the neighbor next to me said, 'They took her children, they took her children!' And I said, 'Where did they take them?' and she said, 'Probably to burn, they will burn them.' And I got scared, thinking, 'this woman has lost her mind. So we are going to lose our minds here?' I didn't believe that one could burn a child alive.*"

"T HEY SENT US *in to have a shower and then they shaved our heads. They gave us the striped uniforms to put on. I had a man's suit and my father quickly rolled up my sleeves and my pants because that's all you had—the striped uniform. That striped uniform I kept until I was liberated. I was with my father—all the men were on one side and the women on the other. Then this woman walked up to me and she asked me how old I was and I said, 'I'm thirteen,' and she said quickly, 'Don't say you're thirteen, say you're seventeen.' She was with the Nazis, with the SS who were walking around. So I told my father and he said, 'Then say you're seventeen if she told you!' That saved my life because the SS were walking around asking everyone, 'How old are you?' I said I was seventeen and this officer looked me up and down and he left me there, left me with my father. That was unbelievable; it was just luck that she walked over to me.*"

Aniela Ania Radek
(Born in Poland, 1926)
Aniela was 15 years old when she was sent to Auschwitz concentration camp.

Peter Hersch
(Born in Czechoslovakia, 1930)
Peter recalls how an SS officer in Auschwitz told him to lie about his age and as a result saved him from the gas chamber.

"WHEN WE GOT into the camp we were introduced to this overseer, who was called a kapo inside the camp. I asked this kapo when we were going to be reunited with our parents. And she pointed to one of the four brick chimneys bellowing fire and soot, and she said, 'Do you see these chimneys?' I said, 'Yes.' She says, 'There go your parents and when you go through the chimneys you'll be reunited.' I turned to my fellow prisoners and I said, 'What is she talking about? What does that mean?' Even in my darkest nightmares I could not have imagined the things that were going on there."

"A WEEK LATER I was selected from my camp to go into another camp. It was then that I was separated from my sister, Clara. But we arranged to meet at the wires every morning at a certain place so that we could wave to each other and tell each other that we are still alive and we're still okay. Before Yom Kippur in 1944, we were worried that something was going to happen because the Nazis always had something in store during holidays or on Sabbath. I went to the wires and my sister didn't show and I thought maybe she was upset because of the holiday and I thought maybe she would be there the following morning. She didn't show then either and when she didn't come the third day I knew that something had happened to her. After the war I found out that there were big selections that day and that she was selected out to be killed."

"ONCE A WEEK the German officers, they used to come in every barrack, they… used to go block to block and tell the women to undress…And one by one they used to pass through them, naked of course, and they were looking at you if you haven't got any disease or anything like that…And the ones that they didn't like, that had something wrong with them, they took the number and they put them in a room, completely separate from the others and then at nighttime they came with a truck, they took them to the gas chamber. That was every week we had to do that!…To live with that fear! Can you imagine? If someone doesn't know when they will die they are not scared, but if you know that you are going to die, that your turn will come, it's a terrible thing."

Renée Firestone
(Born in Czechoslovakia, 1924)
Renée recalls her arrival at
Auschwitz, and the day she feared
her sister had been killed.

Lola Putt
(Born in Greece, 1926)
Lola describes the humiliation
and terror of the weekly
inspections in Auschwitz.

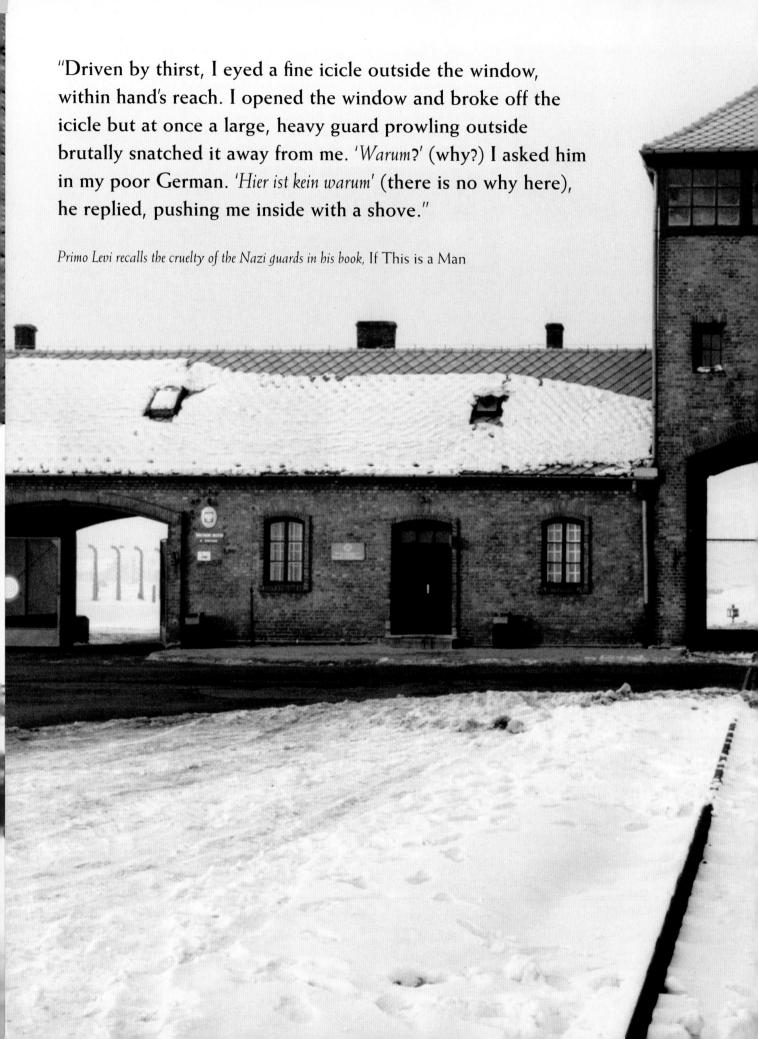

"Driven by thirst, I eyed a fine icicle outside the window, within hand's reach. I opened the window and broke off the icicle but at once a large, heavy guard prowling outside brutally snatched it away from me. *'Warum?'* (why?) I asked him in my poor German. *'Hier ist kein warum'* (there is no why here), he replied, pushing me inside with a shove."

Primo Levi recalls the cruelty of the Nazi guards in his book, If This is a Man

The gates to Auschwitz-Birkenau, photographed in January 1995

JEWISH EFFORTS TO RESCUE JEWS

OUTSIDE EUROPE, Jewish individuals
and groups made attempts to help the
Jews of Europe. They protested against
Nazism, pleaded with governments to
intervene, and provided welfare for
Jews in the ghettos. Some helped Jews
to escape, while others struck deals to
try to end deportations.

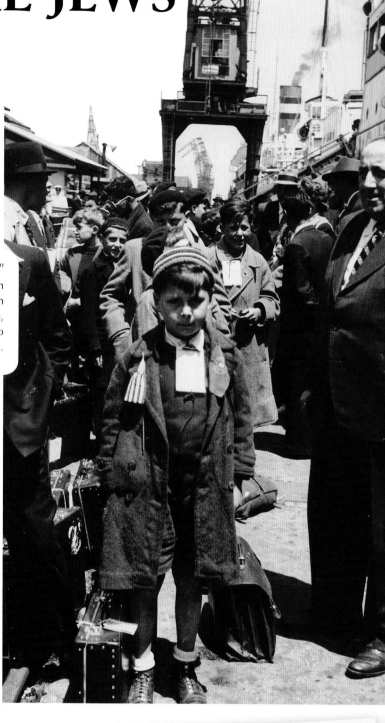

The work of "The Joint"
Between 1939 and 1945, the American Jewish Joint Distribution
Committee—known as "The Joint"—raised more than $70 million
for Holocaust victims, providing welfare, such as orphanages,
schools, and communal kitchens. The Joint also helped Jews to
escape, like this boy about to board a ship in Portugal.

American rabbis
The American rabbis' 'Vaad ha-Hatzala Rescue Committee was
set up in November 1939. By 1941, it had helped 650 rabbis
and Jewish students reach the US, Palestine, and Shanghai,
among other places, and rescued 1,220 Jews from the Terezin
ghetto-camp in Czechoslovakia. Here, in Washington, D.C.,
in 1943, 400 rabbis are marching to demand that President
Roosevelt rescue Jews from Nazi-occupied Europe.

The Bermuda Conference
In April 1943, an international conference discussed the
plight of victims of the Nazis. The Allies, fearing they
might be obliged to take in Jews, agreed not to ask
Germany to release refugees. Britain did not let any more
Jews into Palestine and the US did not change its
immigration laws. A Jewish organization placed this
ad exposing the conference in *The New York Times*.

The Jewish Agency

This organization encouraged Jews to settle in British Palestine. It saved 50,000 Jews through a deal whereby Germany "exported" Jews and seized their money as payment. The agency also organized illegal immigration to Palestine. In 1939, the British confined the 850 refugees from Romania on this ship, the *Parita*.

Saving young Jewish people

An important project of the Jewish Agency was Youth Aliyah (immigration). In 1934, it began to save Jewish children from difficulties and dangers, to educate them and bring them to live in Palestine. Before the Holocaust, about 5,000 were educated in boarding schools and children's villages there. The agency also rescued young people from Nazi Germany, including those here.

HANNAH SZENES

Born in Hungary in 1921, Hannah Szenes believed that the Land of Israel was the real home of the Jewish people and she went to live there at the age of 18. She joined the British Army and bravely volunteered to parachute into Hungary to collect information about Nazi activities and rescue Jews. Although the Nazis captured and tortured her, she never surrendered or betrayed her comrades. The Nazis executed her by firing squad in 1944.

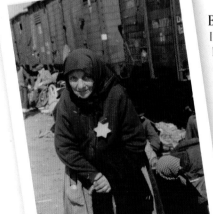

Blood for trucks

In 1944, the Nazi leader Adolf Eichmann and Hungarian Jewish activists Joel and Hansi Brand came up with the idea of "blood for trucks": if the Allies sent the Nazis 10,000 trucks, the Nazis would spare one million Jews and evict them from Europe. But the Allies did not want to help the Nazis win the war by supplying trucks, neither did they want one million Jews. The failure of the deal meant the continued deportation of Hungary's Jews, such as this woman shown here on her arrival at Birkenau.

The Europa Plan

Deportations from Slovakia began in 1942, and these Jews were among those deported. However, when Jewish activists bribed an SS officer with $40,000–$50,000, the deportations ended. They decided to try the idea elsewhere and the Europa Plan was hatched: Jews of the world would pay $2–3 million for the Nazis to end all deportations in Europe. Tragically, the plan failed because Jewish organizations could not get banks to transfer money to Nazi-occupied countries.

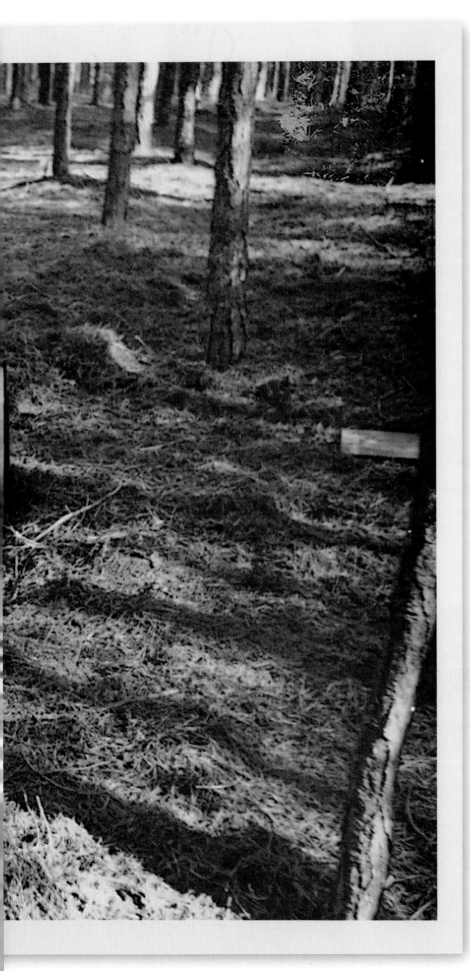

"We removed the Earth and carried it many kilometers away. Then we would steal the doors to a barn, to make the door. We even moved trees onto the top. If anyone saw us, we had to start again."

Eta Wrobel and her father escaped the ghetto liquidation by fleeing into the forest, where they set up a large partisan unit. She survived the war.

Hitler and the Catholic Church
The Roman Catholic Church hoped that
the Third Reich would defeat communism.
Hitler promised not to interfere with the
Church, and Pope Pius XII agreed that
the Church would not comment on Nazi
activities and policies. The Church ignored
Nazi atrocities and, when Jews in Rome
were deported, it broke its pledge to
protect them. This nun is asking for
Hitler's autograph.

THE CHURCHES

CHRISTIANS HAVE OFTEN DEBATED whether they should
be involved in political action to change the world or
concentrate on changing themselves and their relationship
with God. During the Nazi period, especially when the
Third Reich started persecuting minorities, this debate
escalated. Most European churches and individual
Christians took a neutral stance. But some worked
with the Nazis, while others opposed
them, often at cost to their own lives.
Many Christians who rescued
Jews were members of
religious minorities.

Jews and the churches
Any Jews who were protected by a church
had to pose as Christians to avoid being
discovered by the Nazis or betrayed to
them. Sometimes, church congregations
expected the Jews they hid to convert
to Christianity. These two Jews, perhaps
wearing their yellow stars for the last time,
seek refuge in a church. The angle that the
photographer has chosen emphasizes the
perceived size and strength of the church.

"Hidden children"

Some Jewish parents saved their children from deportation by entrusting them to a Christian family or organization. "Hidden children" were instructed in Christian beliefs and always had to hide their Jewish identity. This Jewish girl, pictured with her cousin and a Catholic priest, has received her First Communion as a member of the Church.

Rescued by Quakers

The Quakers (or "Society of Friends") are a religious group that refuses to fight in any war. During the Holocaust, Quakers hid and rescued children, like these Spanish Jewish boys who are helping American Quakers in a French refugee camp. They also saved some French Jews by smuggling them into Switzerland, and took 1,000 Jewish children to the US.

German Christians

The German Evangelical Church was the main Protestant Church in Germany. A group called the German Christians became a Nazi voice within the Church, and its leader Ludwig Müller, giving the Nazi salute above, was given the title of "Reich Bishop" in 1933. German Christians banned non-Aryans from being ministers or Church teachers and fired anyone who had Jewish ancestors.

FIRST THEY CAME...

First the Nazis came for the Communists and I did not speak out—because I was not a Communist.

Then they came for the Socialists and I did not speak out—because I was not a Socialist.

Then they came for the Trade Unionists, and I did not speak out—because I was not a Trade Unionist.

Then they came for the Jews, and I did not speak out—because I was not a Jew.

Then they came for me—and there was no one left to speak out for me.

Pastor Martin Niemöller

The Confessing Church was led by Pastor Martin Niemöller. He said he would rather burn his church to the ground than preach the Nazi trinity of "race, blood, and soil." His statement, above, about taking a stand against injustice has become well known. He was deported to a concentration camp.

Dietrich Bonhoeffer

A leader of the Confessing Church, Dietrich Bonhoeffer believed that Jews should convert to Christianity but courageously opposed the Nazis' plans to murder Jews. This bold bronze sculpture outside his church in Berlin depicts the way the Nazis hanged him in prison, naked and kneeling. He had been captured while helping Jews escape to Switzerland.

VOICES
ENDURING THE DEATH MARCHES

Many thousands of people died during the death marches—enforced walks from the camps that covered huge distances, invariably without food or water. No one could stop to rest. If they did, the Nazis would shoot them on the spot.

"*By now I was accustomed to cruelty. I've seen and heard things happening in Auschwitz and in Birkenau. But what I saw on that march—I will never, never forget. It was pitch dark and we were marching. SS men nearby were watching us. Everyone was afraid because the moment you stepped out of the line, instantaneously you had a bullet in your head, and you just dropped wherever you were. I saw hundreds of people shot—not only Jews—there were Poles, there were people from every nationality, begging and pleading for their lives. But there was absolutely no mercy. You marched or you were dead.*"

"*After marching throughout most of the night, I was prepared any moment just to step aside, I had had enough, I couldn't take it anymore. At that point a gust of wind blew my cap off and so in the bitter cold, my shaven head was completely uncovered. I figured I'm going to collapse any minute anyway so I may as well end my misery. As I was thinking about it, the person marching next to me kept on talking to me, encouraging me, pleading with me not to give up, 'We must survive. We can't let them get away with it.' I was crying that I was cold. Then he saw a corpse on the side with a hat, so he stepped out of the line, took off the hat and gave it to me. He risked his life for me, because he could very easily have been shot, just to make sure that I had a cap. I remember marching, sleeping and marching, and when I eventually opened up my eyes, it was daylight already. I looked around to see if I could see him but the man was gone and I was again alone and just going on like a robot.*"

Mayer Schondorf
(Born in Czechoslovakia, 1928)
In 1945 Mayer was sent on a death march to Gross Rosen camp from Auschwitz-Birkenau.

"*THEN THEY TOOK us on this march, which really was a death march. They were deliberately shooting us from the front, from the back, from everywhere so there would be less people, and anybody that stayed behind a little bit, that couldn't walk so fast, they just shot him and left him in the gutter. I didn't know how far it was but since then I found out it was about 30 kilometers or 30 miles, I'm not sure which, from Gusen to Gunskirchen…You can imagine…we were dead tired from walking for miles and miles and miles, we slept always in the open…And the shooting was all night long. Shooting at us nonstop…And in the morning when they said, 'Eintreten!' ['Get up!'] I pushed my friend next to me, that I knew, that we walked together, to get up—he was dead, he was shot.*"

"*WE WENT THROUGH towns. We begged for a piece of food or water from the people—they saw us marching and they must have known the end was coming, yet nobody lifted a finger, nobody—that's something that you don't forget.*"

"*IF A person couldn't walk, or even just tripped, they shot him and left him lying there, but you kept going because you didn't dare stop to find out if the person was dead or not. We kept on walking and if you had to go to the bathroom, well, unfortunately, as primitive and as awful as it sounds, you just went in your pants and you kept on walking. So my mother and my sister and myself, we walked. One of us would be in the middle and the other two took the one in the middle under the armpits, so you were half dragged along by the other two and you could close your eyes and sort of doze off. The three of us rotated, but I think I was the one who got most benefit of this protection because I just couldn't stay awake. We were housed overnight in a barn, which had an awful lot of hay. Finally we could lie down—it didn't matter where and how—and fall asleep.*"

Peter Hersch
(Born in Czechoslovakia, 1930)
In 1945, Peter was sent on a death march to the Gunskirchen concentration camp.

Vera Eden
(Born in Czechoslovakia, 1930)
Vera recalls how her mother and her sister helped her to keep walking on a march to Gross Rosen.

CRISIS MANAGEMENT

THE WORLD HAD NEVER faced such a complex and large-scale crisis as the Holocaust. The Allies had to cope with the tragedy while still fighting the war. Military chaplains and relief agencies played important roles in the immediate tasks of rescuing survivors and controlling the spread of disease. Liberators also collected evidence to be used in the trials of Nazi war criminals.

Medical checkups and care
Disease was rampant in all the camps, and those who managed to survive were weak from lack of food. Some inmates had suffered injuries as well. Doctors and nurses visited all the camps to carry out medical assessments and determine the treatments that were needed. This Soviet physician is examining survivors at Auschwitz.

Helping the hungry
Feeding programs were a priority. Some survivors did not have the strength to eat and nurses had to feed them by spoon. Soldiers initially gave out chocolate and cannned meat, unaware that rich food would be a shock to the system and that overfeeding could kill the malnourished.

Disease and disinfection
The camps were overrun with rodents and infested with bugs. Many survivors were riddled with lice and suffered from typhus or other bacterial infections. These women at Bergen-Belsen are being sprayed with disinfectant to prevent the spread of disease. Delousing was also a priority.

Burying the bodies
Corpses were scattered around the camps and the liberators buried them quickly to avoid disease and distress. Using the same tools as the Nazis—shovels, wheelbarrows, and bulldozers—they buried bodies in mass graves, such as this at Bergen-Belsen.

was s
famil
send
you
I wo
it is
tie,
apa

Le
For
a n
In
Rel
pro
Lar
pe
hel

Cu
Soc
the
arr
reb
enj
as
the

Julia I
(Born
Julia r
decidi
States

Accusing and attacking
For some time, the liberators held Nazi guards as prisoners in the same camps, and their victims found this overwhelmingly difficult. Some called their torturers insulting names or lashed out at them. This survivor at Buchenwald is identifying a guard who beat the prisoners brutally. They are both still wearing the same uniforms they wore before liberation.

Making the Germans see
The Allies wanted to confront German people with evidence of Nazi crimes so they could never say they did not know. This German woman is horrified at the sight and smell of people murdered by the SS near Namering, Germany. American liberators gave locals camp "tours" to see the evidence for themselves.

Making the Germans work
The Allies forced any Nazis still in camp to work. This served a practical purpose, since urgent jobs were finished more quickly and the Nazis were punished in the process. Here, British soldiers at Bergen-Belsen have ordered local women to bury the Jewish dead. German civilians were also made to dig graves and bury bodies.

151

COUNTING THE COSTS

THE NUMBER OF COMMUNITIES and institutions destroyed in the Holocaust is fairly easy to count, but the effect of their loss is hard to measure. The figures of 10 million people killed—including six million Jews—are often quoted. In truth, the exact figures may never be known because so much evidence was lost. Hitler, for example, burned his papers before he committed suicide. There are countless victims of the Holocaust whose stories may be lost forever.

The Czech Memorial scrolls
Fearing that deserted Czech synagogues would be plundered, Jewish leaders in Prague proposed to the occupying Nazis that religious treasures be brought to Prague's Jewish Museum. These included many Torah scrolls, which ended up in an abandoned synagogue after the war. In 1964, a deal with the Czech authorities brought 1,564 scrolls to Westminster Synagogue in London, England. Over the next 40 years, most scrolls were returned to synagogues across the world.

Recording evidence
The Nazis valued efficiency and precision, so they kept very detailed records of their actions, including official photographs. Individual Nazis would often take photographs of other Nazis abusing their victims and save them as personal mementos. The German filmmaker Leni Riefenstahl (above) made propaganda films for the Nazis, but later some of her films would be used as evidence of Nazi plans.

Evidence destroyed
Toward the end of the war, the Nazis tried to cover up crimes that might bring them shame. They burned Treblinka, for example, and planted potatoes on the site. Evidence was also lost when camps were looted. The Allies burned buildings to stop disease from spreading, such as here at Bergen-Belsen, in Germany, where there was typhus.

Numbers of Jews killed

- none
- 0–1,000
- 1,001–10,000
- 10,001–100,000
- 100,001–1,000,000
- more than 1,000,000

Deaths during the Holocaust

This map gives the figures for Jewish deaths. Other groups selected for death are not included here simply because there are no reliable figures. These include: Soviet prisoners of war—3.3 million estimated, Romanies—figures vary from 250,000 to 1 million, homosexuals—unknown, but 5,000 and 15,000 sent to camps, and Jehovah's Witnesses—1,400 estimated.

NORWAY 728
SWEDEN
FINLAND 11
IRELAND
GREAT BRITAIN
DENMARK 77
ESTONIA 1,000
LATVIA 80,000
MEMEL 8,000
LITHUANIA 135,000
NETHERLANDS 106,000
FREE CITY OF DANZIG 1,000
SOVIET UNION 1,000,000
BELGIUM 24,387
GERMANY 160,000
POLAND 3,000,000
LUXEMBOURG 700
FRANCE 83,000
CZECHOSLOVAKIA 217,000
RUTHENIA 60,000
BUKOVINA 124,632
SWITZERLAND
AUSTRIA 65,000
HUNGARY 200,000
NORTHERN TRANSYLVANIA 105,000
BESSARABIA 200,000
PORTUGAL
SPAIN
ITALY 8,000
YUGOSLAVIA 60,000
ROMANIA 40,000
BULGARIA
MACEDONIA 7,122
THRACE 4,221
ALBANIA 200
TURKEY
GREECE 65,000
KOS 120
RHODES 1,700
CRETE 260

0 km 500 1,000 1,500
0 miles 500 1,000

THE LOSS OF LIFE

In many ways, numbers, especially very large numbers, mean nothing to us. What matters is each and every human being who was murdered by the Nazis. Each had a name, a family, a hometown, and a culture. Each had a past and a present—and would have had a future. Each had his or her own hopes and fears, as well as memories and dreams. Just like Settela Steinbach, a Romany girl, pictured here looking out from a transport wagon on its way to Auschwitz concentration camp, Poland, in 1943.

Loss of learning

All that remains of the once majestic synagogue of Tarnów, Poland, is the central structure, now set in a park. Thousands of synagogues, Jewish schools, and community centers were destroyed in the Holocaust and, with them, much of the learning and laughter that had been at the heart of Jewish life in Eastern Europe.

Access to evidence

After the war, the German government made an archive from surviving Nazi records, but only the Red Cross had permission to see it. However, Germany came under pressure to give access to everyone and in 2006 the world's largest Holocaust archive, the International Tracing Service, opened. The racks hold 50 million records detailing Nazi victims of the Holocaust.

VOICES
SURVIVORS LOOK BACK

In spite of the millions who died, many of those who survived the darkest hours of the Holocaust went on to live full lives around the world. However, such cruelty and suffering is unforgettable, and for most of these survivors one question that remains in their minds today is "Why did this happen?"

"I'VE GOT THREE children—two boys and a girl...I'm very happy, very proud. So there you are, out of where I was—to come to this! It's my greatest joy. So God was good to me...With all the troubles that I've had in life, this makes up for it because I've got a wonderful life with my family and that's all that counts... What the Germans did to us—I can't forget, I can't forget. I can't for the life of me understand how it could have happened. I cannot understand, I don't know, I just don't know."

"I CAN'T BLAME all the Germans and the young generations—how can I say it's their fault? I can't! But I've never been back to Germany since then, since I left it. I do want to before I die; I do want to go back. And my sister wants to go back to Auschwitz to say Kaddish for my parents and my brothers and sister because that's where they died. But other than that I have no interest to go back to Germany and the other places. I have no desire to go back. None whatsoever."

Peter Hersch
(Born in Czechoslovakia, 1930)
Peter struggles to understand why the Holocaust happened and expresses his love for his family.

"*MY CHILDREN WANTED to know about the number on my arm and naturally they were talking about what happened to the Jews because they wanted to know, 'Where are Grandma and Grandpa?' So I told them just in a capsule way what happened to us. I explained to them where I came from and all that but nothing in detail.*"

"*I HAVE TO convince myself that there is a reason for everything. Because otherwise I would say, 'Why did God give the strength to Hitler, to commit this murder act, to annihilate six million Jews and others at the same time? Why was he granted that power since he was an evil man? Why?' That answer nobody can give me.*"

"*PEOPLE CAME to these wires when they could not bear anymore the suffering and the hunger and the starvation. Every morning you could see people hanging from these wires committing suicide, ending their lives. I'm looking at these today and it's hard to believe—if these poles could tell the stories of the things that happened here. It couldn't be true, we keep saying to ourselves, it couldn't be true. Yet we all are marked, we all have the numbers on our arms which tells us that, yes, we were here...I learned something here but I wonder whether the world learned anything. The way you look around the world today you wonder—what did we learn from the Holocaust? What did we learn from this place?...Look at this place. Look at the size of it! Can you imagine the millions that perished here?*"

Diana Golden
(Born in Greece, 1922)
After the war, Diana immigrated to the United States. Like many other survivors, she wonders how the Holocaust happened.

Renée Firestone
(Born in Czechoslovakia, 1924)
Many years after she immigrated to the United States, Renée returned to Auschwitz to visit the memorial site.

167

THE SITES OF THE CAMPS TODAY

VERY LITTLE REMAINS OF MOST CAMPS, which were deliberately demolished or left to decay over time. As the map of Europe changes, so do the politics of the places where the camps stand and opinions on how the sites should be managed. There are strong feelings about how some groups stamp their religious or political mark on both the camps and the memory of those who perished. Auschwitz is now a World Heritage Site and in 2006 the Polish government asked for it to be called "Former Nazi German Concentration Camp of Auschwitz."

Pilgrim or tourist?
Former concentration camps, especially Auschwitz in Poland, attract a large number of visitors. Some come as pilgrims, some as students, and some as tourists. Visitors are sometimes horrified that Auschwitz has become so commercialized, and even has hotdog stands outside. For some, the presence of large crowds of noisy people is insensitive. Visitors often pose to have their photo taken here, under the famous *Arbeit Macht Frei* (Work Brings Freedom) sign.

The "railroad" at Treblinka
In 1943, the Nazis destroyed the camp and railroad line at Treblinka in Poland. However, after the Holocaust, Soviet authorities erected a huge slab saying "Never Again" in many languages. There are also hundreds of standing stones, representing a town or city which was once home to the victims, and the symbolic blocks (above) mark the path of the railroad.

As it was
A few camps were not destroyed by the Nazis or the Allies. At Auschwitz and Majdanek, some barracks, gas chambers, crematoria, and other buildings are still standing. They give some insight into the nature of daily life in the camps, such as the sleeping arrangements in this barrack at Majdanek. But the wooden barracks are slowly rotting away and will eventually fall apart.

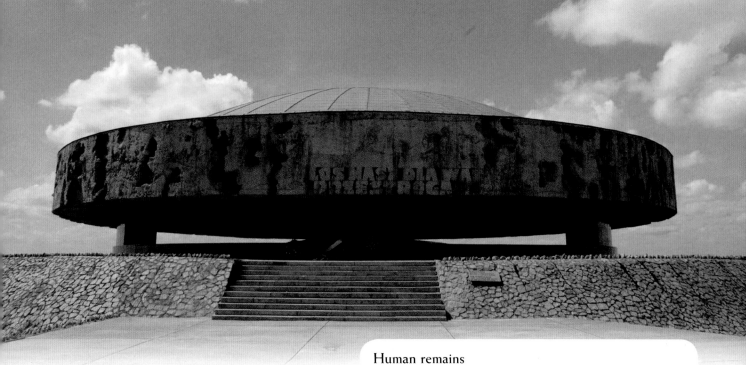

More than a million people visit the site of the former concentration camp at Auschwitz every year.

Human remains
The sites of the concentration camps are effectively huge cemeteries, where the remains of an unknown and mostly nameless number of people lie. To visit a camp is to step on invisible graves. In some camps, ashes have been gathered together and marked. This mausoleum at Majdanek in Poland contains ashes from the nearby crematorium. The Polish inscription reads "Let our fate be a warning for you."

Crosses at Auschwitz
The first Christian crosses appeared at Auschwitz-Birkenau in 1979, when the Polish pope, John Paul II, celebrated Mass there. In 1988, nuns placed the first of many crosses at Auschwitz I, where they had converted the building formerly used to store Zyklon B gas into a convent. Jewish groups protested against the crosses and the location of the convent. In 1993 the nuns left, but the crosses still remain.

Soviet influences
When Poland was a communist country, Soviet influences on political life were very strong. The Soviet Union was proud of the defeat of Nazism and erected many monuments, like this one at the former labor camp of Plaszow in Poland. They were usually huge slabs that symbolized Soviet power. Memorial markers referred to the "victims of fascism," but not to Jews or Romanies.

Memorial stones
All former concentration camps have plaques or markers, and most also display sculptures or installations commemorating the dead. In some camps there are natural stones placed as symbolic gravestones at the spot of a mass grave. Here, at Buchenwald in Germany, the names of the camps where Nazis murdered Romanies are carved into some of the stones. They include Buchenwald itself.

STORIES OF THE SURVIVORS

Alexander Van Kollem

Born in 1928 in Amsterdam, the Netherlands, Alexander's family was interned in Vught transit camp. His father's boss got the family back to Amsterdam, where they went into hiding. He was liberated from the last hiding place by the British in May 1945, but both his parents died at Auschwitz. After the war he returned to Amsterdam before immigrating to the US, where he married in 1952.

Aniela Ania Radek

Born in Poland in 1926, Aniela is a Roman Catholic. In 1941 she was sent to Auschwitz in Poland. After escaping, she went into hiding in a farmhouse near Augsberg. Meanwhile, her father had been killed in France for criticizing the communists. Aniela went to the Sorbonne in France and later to college in Montreal, Canada. She married in Toronto in 1954 and has one daughter.

Bernard Schuster

Born in Poland in 1928, Bernard's father died before the war and his mother was shot trying to escape from one of the ghettos. Bernard went into hiding and was later liberated by the Russians from the woods near Jasionowka in Poland. He went into Santa Cesarea Displaced Persons' camp in Italy from 1945–47, before immigrating to New York. He studied law at Harvard and works with the US Jewish community.

Eric Richmond

Born in Vienna in 1924, Eric fled Austria in 1938 as part of the *Kindertransport* and came to England. During the war he made army boots and years later become a restaurateur and hotelier. In 1970 he went back to visit Austria, but only very briefly. His father and mother were both killed during the war. He married in Germany in 1963 and has one daughter. He now lives in England.

Felicia Carmelly

Born in Romania in 1931, Felicia was sent to Shargorod ghetto in Transnistria, Ukraine, in 1941, where she worked in the fields until 1944. She was liberated by the Soviet army in 1944 and returned to Romania before immigrating to Canada. She has one daughter. Felicia went on to earn a Ph.D. in Psychology and to publish a book. She is the founder of the Transnistria Survivors' Association of Toronto.

Fred Spiegel

Fred was born in Germany in 1932; his mother immigrated to England in the hope of sending for Fred and his sister later. However, war broke out and Fred was sent to Bergen-Belsen, via Westerbork, and was eventually liberated by the Americans. After the war he traveled to England, Chile, Israel, and the US. His mother and sister survived the war. Fred is married with three children.

The people who are quoted throughout the book on the Voices pages are introduced here. Their incredible stories of strength and survival provide a moving testimony to the power of the human spirit.

Claire Boren

Born in Poland in 1938, Claire and her family were sent to Mizoch ghetto in 1942, and then went into hiding. Initially, she was hidden in an attic. Later, helped by a Baptist farmer, she and her mother hid in a hole beneath a pigsty for three months. She was liberated by the Soviet army in early 1944. She then went to Eshwege Displaced Persons' camp from 1946–49 before immigrating to the US.

Diana Golden

Born in 1922 on the Greek island of Rhodes, Diana and her family were transported to a concentration camp near Athens in 1944, after the Germans occupied the island. The family was then sent to Auschwitz. Her father died on the way and she never saw her mother again. She was later sent to Terezin, where she was liberated by the Soviets. After the war Diana started a new life in the US.

Emma Mogilensky

Born in Germany in 1923, Emma fled in 1939 and caught a train to London, where she joined the British Army, working as a cook. In 1950 she immigrated to the US, where she met her husband. In 1992 she visited her hometown of Cronheim in Germany. Both her parents were killed in the Holocaust but her brother escaped and now also lives in the US. She has three children.

Henry Greenblatt

Born in Poland in 1930, Henry's parents and sister were killed in 1942. He spent time in the Warsaw ghetto before moving to Siedlce ghetto. In 1942, on a death march from Siedlce, he managed to escape and went into hiding under a false identity, working on a farm from 1943–46, and as part of the resistance for the Home Army of Poland. Henry now lives in the US.

Henry Oster

Born in 1928 in Germany, Henry and his family were deported to Łódź ghetto in Poland in 1941, where Henry's father died of malnutrition. In 1943, Henry and his mother were deported to Auschwitz, where he was separated from his mother, whom he never saw again. At the end of 1944, he was sent on a death march to Buchenwald, where he remained until liberation by the Americans in 1945.

Julia Lentini

Born in 1926 in Biedenkopf, Germany, to a Romany family, Julia and her family were arrested in 1943 and sent to Auschwitz, where both her parents died. She was moved to Schlieben camp in 1945, where she was later liberated by the Soviets. After the war she was housed as a war refugee near Biedenkopf. She later met and married an American soldier and they immigrated to the US in 1946.

BIG QUESTIONS

LEARNING ABOUT THE HOLOCAUST answers many questions, but many more remain … Can someone who did wrong really say, "I was only obeying orders"? Should we judge how people behaved in the Holocaust, such as the victims who did not resist the Nazis or people who did not help? What about buying goods from "Nazi" companies or using medicines developed by Nazi doctors? Should we forgive? Can we forget? What can we do so that nothing like the Holocaust ever happens again?

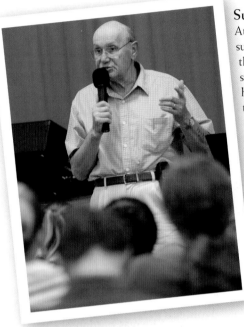

Survivors speak
At first, very few Holocaust survivors could talk about their suffering, especially to strangers. But when they heard people denying that the Holocaust happened, many of them felt they had to speak out. A school in Tennessee invited this survivor to speak to the children. The children discovered that meeting and learning about one person is more valuable than learning facts about millions.

The churches and the Holocaust
Although there are churches that still preach traditional beliefs about Jews, some have revised their views. Jewish-Christian relations are now closer than in recent decades. In 2006, Pope Benedict XVI visited Auschwitz (left). The previous Pope, John Paul II, also visited the camp, and apologized for the fact that Christian beliefs had caused Jewish suffering.

Holocaust denial
Despite the facts about the Holocaust, there are still anti-Semitic individuals and groups who claim that it never happened, or that it has been exaggerated. In Britain in 2000, Holocaust denier David Irving lost his court case against historian Deborah Lipstadt (above) and her publishing company, in which he accused them of libel (slander).

Lessons not learned

More than 60 years after the Holocaust, nothing has happened on quite the same scale. Yet there is still rampant racism and acts of genocide in many parts of the world. In Europe and North America neo (new) Nazi groups adopt the language and the style of the Nazis, as in this demonstration in Olympia, Washington.

Making good again

Not all Nazis were German. Not all Germans were Nazis. Germany has repealed Nazi laws and changed Nazi political and social systems in a process called de-Nazification. It has also made moves to rectify what it did wrong through various projects. Many young Germans feel responsible for what their country did. This group is part of a project to restore Jewish cemeteries in Eastern Europe.

Never again

The horrors of the Holocaust make many individuals and groups determined to work for a more loving and peaceful world, and to prevent any further genocide. In addition, some Jewish individuals and groups realize that there is a need to defend the Jewish community. The slogan on this girl's T-shirt—Never Again—affirms the commitment to stop anything like the Holocaust from ever happening again.

Voices from the past

In 1942, 14-year-old Petr Gens was deported to Theresienstadt. He was interested in astronomy and science, and also liked art. His drawing *Moon Landscape* shows his view of Earth from the cratered Moon. He drew the Earth as the Moon appears to us—peaceful and full of light. In 1944, Petr was murdered at Auschwitz. His drawing survives to challenge and inspire us.

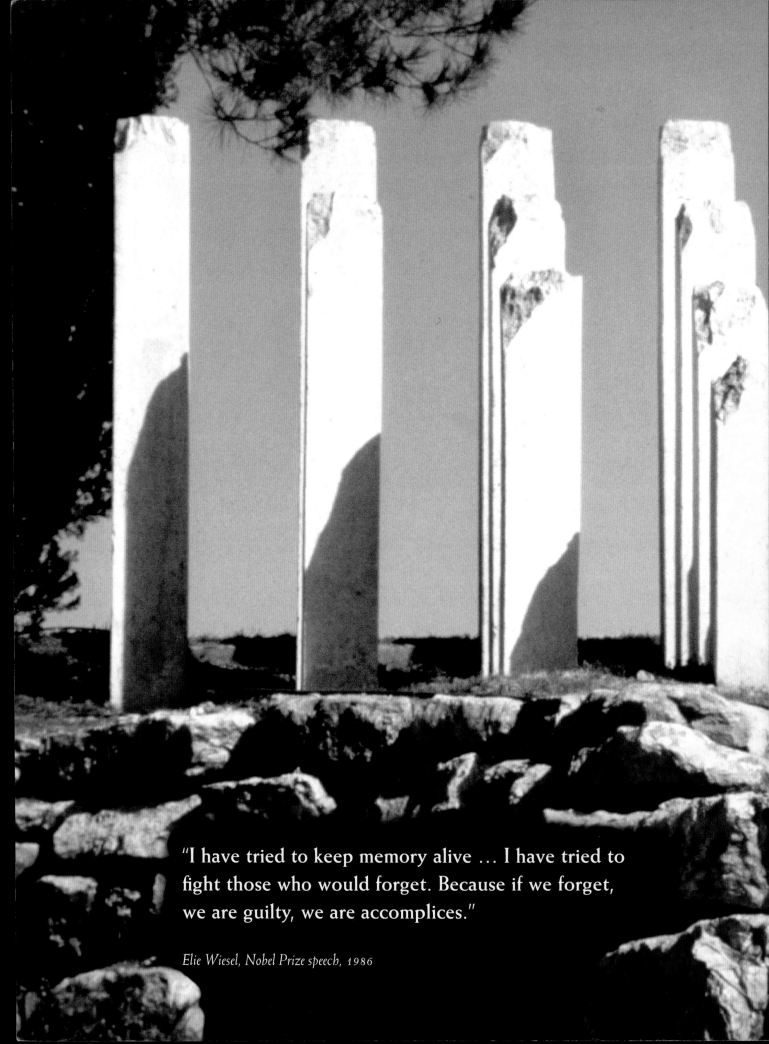

"I have tried to keep memory alive ... I have tried to fight those who would forget. Because if we forget, we are guilty, we are accomplices."

Elie Wiesel, Nobel Prize speech, 1986

The forest of steles (slabs of stone) at the entrance to the Hall of Murdered Children, at Israel's national Holocaust memorial, Yad Vashem

The nations that joined with Britain to fight Nazi Germany during World War II, including the Soviet Union, the US, and France.

Annex
To add new land to existing territory.

Anschluss
Term used to describe the German takeover of Austria in 1938, from the German word meaning "join."

Anti-Semitism
A form of racism based on hatred of, and prejudice against, Jews.

Aryan
The term the Nazis used to describe people who they believed were of pure German blood—a superior race of white people, with blond hair and blue eyes.

Axis Powers
Name given to the alliance of Germany and Italy, and later Japan, during World War II.

Blitzkreig
German for "lightning war"—an intense military campaign intended to bring swift results. The term "The Blitz" was used to describe German air raids on London in 1940–41.

Communism
The political theory that advocates a society in which all property is publicly owned and each person is paid according to his or her needs. A supporter is known as a communist.

Concentration camp
A prison camp set up for holding large numbers of political prisoners.

Crematorium
A building with large ovens for burning dead bodies.

Czechoslovakia
Until 1993, the two nations now known as the Czech Republic and Slovakia were united as the country of Czechoslovakia. Between 1939 and 1945, Czechoslovakia was split into Bohemia and Moravia, and Slovakia.

Death camp
A camp set up to exterminate inmates quickly and efficiently.

Displaced Person (DP)
A person who is left with no country to go to after a war.

Nazi mobile killing squads, set up by the SS to follow the German army as they conquered land in Eastern Europe, and round up and kill Jews.

Emancipation
A period of freedom from traditional ideas, also the state of being free from restrictions or control.

Enlightenment
The 18th-century European philosophy emphasizing reason and individualism rather than tradition.

Fascism
A system of strong government by a leader with powerful appeal, who is dedicated to the rebirth of a nation. A supporter is known as a Fascist.

Final Solution
The Nazi term for the plan to exterminate the Jews of Europe—the solution to what they believed was the "Jewish problem."

Führer
The German word meaning "leader" applied to Hitler.

General Government
The name given to the areas of Poland occupied by Germany in 1939, but not incorporated into the Third Reich.

Genocide
The deliberate attempt to destroy a national, religious, racial, or ethnic group, in whole or in part.

Gentile
A person who is not Jewish.

Gestapo
The secret police of Nazi Germany.

Ghetto
An area of a city where Jews were forced to live in cramped, inhumane conditions during Nazi rule.

Hebrew
The language spoken in Israel today. Also, the name for a member of the tribe that originated in ancient Palestine.

Holocaust
The mass murder of the Jews, and other minorities, by the Nazis between 1933 and 1945.

Israel
The modern Jewish state in the Middle East, established in 1948. The "Land of Israel" is also the traditional name for the ancient Hebrew nation (c. 930–721 BCE).

A Jewish council set up by the Nazis to run
ghetto communities during World War II.

Kapo
A concentration camp prisoner who
supervised other prisoners, for which he
or she received privileges.

Kindertransport
The mass evacuation of children from Germany
to Britain in 1938.

Kristallnacht
From the German, meaning "Night of Broken
Glass," the night of violence against Jews and
Jewish property on November, 9–10, 1938.

Labor camp
A prison camp in which inmates are subjected
to enforced hard labor.

Middle Ages
The period of European history between
the 5th and 15th centuries. Also known as the
medieval period.

Nazi Party
The National Socialist German Workers' Party,
led by Hitler. The Party believed in strong
military leadership to enforce nationalistic,
racist, and anti-Semitic policies.

Palestine
Traditionally, the area of the Middle East that
once included the countries now called Israel
and Jordan. Today, Palestine is made up of areas
of the West Bank and Gaza.

Partisan
A resistance fighter operating behind
enemy lines.

Pogrom
An organized, often officially encouraged,
attack on a minority group.

Propaganda
Information—sometimes false or partly false—
used to influence the opinions of others.

Putsch
A sudden attempt at political revolution or a
violent uprising, from the German word for
"thrust" or "blow."

The German Parliament.

Reparations
To make amends for a wrong-doing, and also
the payment of compensation by a defeated
nation for war damages.

Republic
A state in which power is held by the people or
their elected representatives, not by a monarch.

Revolution
The overthrow of a government or social order
by force.

Romany
The name for a nomadic group of people, often
referred to by the derogatory term of "Gypsies."

Shtetl
A small Jewish town or village in Eastern
Europe or Russia.

Sinti
A nomadic people of Europe, closely related to
the Romany.

Social democracy
The political belief in moving gradually and
peacefully to a system of socialism (state
ownership) by democratic (system of free
elections) means. A supporter is known as a
social democrat.

Sonderkommando
Prisoners of death camps who were forced to
remove dead bodies in the gas chambers for
cremation or burial. From the German word
sonder, meaning "special."

Soviet Union
The name given to the Russian Empire after
the revolution of 1917, and short for the
Union of Soviet Socialist Republics (USSR).
In 1991, when the Soviet Union collapsed, the
area became known as the Commonwealth of
Independent States (CIS).

SS
From the German *Schutzstaffel*, meaning
"protective squad." The SS began as Hitler's
personal guard but grew to become a large and
powerful organization responsible for
concentration camps and racial matters.

Also known as Brown shirts, a force of troops
used by the Nazi party to help Hitler rise
to power.

Synagogue
A building used for Jewish religious study,
worship, and celebration.

Third Reich
The period of German government from 1933–
45, from the German meaning "Third Empire."

Torah
The Jewish sacred writings, used in synagogues
in the form of scrolls.

Transit camp
A camp where inmates are held temporarily
before being moved on.

USSR (see Soviet Union)

Vichy France
The area of southern France occupied by
Germany between 1942 and1945.

Yiddish
The traditional language of the
Jews of Eastern Europe, based on German,
Hebrew, and several modern languages
including Polish and Russian.

Zionism
The movement for the reestablishment and the
development of a Jewish nation in the area that
is now Israel.

GLOSSARY

INDEX

CREDITS

CREDITS AND ACKNOWLEDGMENTS

The David S. Wyman Institute for Holocaust Studies Washington D.C: (cl). 119 Bildarchiv Preußischer Kulturbesitz, Berlin: (tl). Government Press Office: Fritz Cohen (tr). United States Holocaust Memorial Museum: Courtesy of Musée de la Resistance et de la Deportation (br); Courtesy of Beit Hannah Senesh (cl). Courtesy of photo archive, Yad Vashem: (bl). 120 Corbis: Bettmann (bl). Wiener Library: (br). 121 United States Holocaust Memorial Museum: Courtesy of Sigmund Baum (tr); Courtesy of Frihedsmuseet (tl); Jewish Historical Museum of Yugoslavia (bl); Courtesy of Gavra Mandil (br). 124 United States Holocaust Memorial Museum: Courtesy of Mert Bland (cl); Courtesy of Hiroki Sugihara (bc); Courtesy of Thomas Veres, Photo by Thomas Veres (br). 124-125 Courtesy of photo archive, Yad Vashem: Yad Vashem Artifacts Collection. Gift of the Pacifici family, Italy (t). 125 Getty Images: Hulton Archive (cr). United States Holocaust Memorial Museum: Leopold Page Photograph Collection (bl). Courtesy of photo archive, Yad Vashem: (tr). 126-127 United States Holocaust Memorial Museum: Courtesy of Bep Meyer Zion. 130 Bavarian State Library, Munich: (t). Courtesy of photo archive, Yad Vashem: (b). 131 akg-images: (tr) (br). United States Holocaust Memorial Museum: Courtesy of Hanna Meyer-Moses (tc); Courtesy of Beatrice Muchman (tl). Corbis: Bettmann (bl). Science Photo Library: Volker Steger (br). 133 British Pathé Ltd: (br). Corbis: Bettmann (t). United States Holocaust Memorial Museum: Courtesy of National Archives and Records Administration, College Park (c). 134 akg-images: (bl): © Alexandra Szyk Bracie (tl). 134-135 © Beit Lohamei Haghetaot/The Ghetto Fighters House Museum: family of Jacob Davidson. 135 © Beit Lohamei Haghetaot/The Ghetto Fighters House Museum: (cra); family of Jacob Davidson (br). United States Holocaust Memorial Museum: (cr). Courtesy of photo archive, Yad Vashem: (tc). 136 © Alexandre Oler: as published in Witness, Images of Auschwitz with illustrations by David Olère and text by Alexandre Oler, 1998 WESTWIND PRESS. 137 akg-images: (c). Florida Center for Instructional Technology: (t). United States Holocaust Memorial Museum: (bl). Courtesy of photo archive, Yad Vashem: (br). 138-139 United States Holocaust Memorial Museum: Courtesy of National Archives and Records Administration, College Park. 140 Imperial War Museum: (cr). TopFoto: (tl). United States Holocaust Memorial Museum: Courtesy of Archiwum Panstwowego Muzeum na Majdanku (c). 141 akg-images: Benno Gantner (bl); Ullstein Bild (tr). Corbis: (r). United States Holocaust Memorial Museum: Courtesy of Albert Abramson (tr); Courtesy of Seymour Schenkman (bc). 144 akg-images. 145 akg-images: (tl) (br). (c) Canadian War Museum (CWM): (cr). Collection of the Yad Vashem Art Museum, Jerusalem: Zinovii Tolkatchev (1903-1977) A Mother and her Baby, Auschwitz, 1945 Pencil on paper. Gift of Anel Tolkatcheva and Ilya Tolkatchev, Kiev (bl). 146-147 Getty Images: Hulton Archive. 150 akg-images: (tr) (br). United States Holocaust Memorial Museum: Courtesy of Dr. Robert G. Waits (c). Courtesy of photo archive, Yad Vashem: (bl). 151 akg-images: Ullstein Bild (bl). Corbis: Bettmann (br); Hulton-Deutsch Collection (t). 152 Collection of the Yad Vashem Art Museum, Jerusalem: Yad Vashem Art Museum, Gift of Sigmund A. Rolat, New York, in loving memory of his parents, Henryk ans Mania, who perished in the Holocaust (cr). 153 United States Holocaust Memorial Museum: (cl); Courtesy of George Kadish/Zvi Kadushin (cr); Courtesy of Leah Lahav (t); Courtesy of Ruchana Medine White (b). 154 United States Holocaust Memorial Museum: Courtesy of George Kadish/Zvi Kadushin (bl); Courtesy of Alice Lev (c); Courtesy of Regina Gutman Speigel (tl). 154-155 United States Holocaust Memorial Museum: Courtesy of Chaia Libstug-Rosenblum (b). 155 United States Holocaust Memorial Museum: Courtesy of Inge Berner (tr); Courtesy of George Kadish/Zvi Kadushin (tl); Courtesy of Diane Popowski (br); Courtesy of Yivo Institute for Jewish Research (tc); HIAS Archives: (bl). 156 Photo courtesy of HIAS Archives: (tl). United States Holocaust Memorial Museum: Courtesy of Schaja and Pnina Klein (bl); Courtesy of Bernard Marks (c). 157 Getty Images: AFP (t); Time Life Pictures (bl). United States Holocaust Memorial Museum: Courtesy of Elinor Gabriel (br). 160-161 Corbis: Michael St. Maur Sheil. 162 Czech Memorial Scrolls Trust: (cl). Getty Images: (c); Olympic Museum/Allsport (tr). United States Holocaust Memorial Museum: Courtesy of Hadassah Bimko Rosensaft (b). 163 Getty Images: Ralph Orlowski (bl). Angela Gluck Wood: (br). © Beit Lohamei Haghetaot/The Ghetto Fighters House Museum: (tl). Central Zionist Archives, Jerusalem: (b). John C. Menszer: (cr). 165 Corbis: Henny Ray Abrams/Reuters (br).

Tamara Deuel: (tl). United States Holocaust Memorial Museum: Courtesy of Lilo Plaschkes (bl). Collection of the Yad Vashem Art Museum, Jerusalem: Yehuda Bacon (b.1929) In Memory of the Czech Transport to the Gas Chambers, 1945. Charcoal on paper. Loan of the artist (tr). 168 Alamy Images: Popperfoto (bl). Getty Images: Time Life Pictures (t). United States Holocaust Memorial Museum: Courtesy of National Archives and Records Administration, College Park (br). 169 Corbis: Bettmann (t). Getty Images: Gjon Mili/Time & Life Pictures (bl). Le Monde: Plantu (br). 172 Corbis: Bettmann (bl). United States Holocaust Memorial Museum: Courtesy of National Archives and Records Administration, College Park (br). 172-173 akg-images: Licensed by DACS, 2007 (tc). 173 Corbis: Bettmann (br). Getty Images: Timothy Clary/ AFP (tr). United States Holocaust Memorial Museum: Corbis-Bettmann (cr); Courtesy of Benjamin Ferencz (bl). 174 Angela Gluck Wood: (t) (bl) (br). 175 akg-images: Ullstein Bild (br). Getty Images: Piotr Malecki (bl). Angela Gluck Wood: (t). Stan Kujawa: Photographersdirect.com (tr). 176 Corbis: Reuters (t). Angela Gluck Wood: (cl). 176-177 Corbis: Fabrizio Bensch/Pool/EPA (b). 177 Alamy Images: pbpgalleries (tr). Holocaust Resource Center - Temple Judea of Manhasset: (br). Dina Koren: Photographersdirect.com (tl). 182 Empics Ltd: Adam Butler/AP (br); Diether Endlicher/AP (bl); Mark Gilliland/AP (t). 183 Action Reconciliation Service for Peace, Berlin: David Grodzki (cl). Empics Ltd: Elaine Thompson/AP (tr). Angela Gluck Wood: (cr). Collection of the Yad Vashem Art Museum, Jerusalem: Petr Ginz (1928-1944) Moon Landscape, 1942-1944 Pencil on paper. Gift of Otto Ginz, Haifa (b). 184-185 akg-images: Juergen Sorges.

Jacket images: *Front*: PunchStock: Stockbyte Platinum

All other images © Dorling Kindersley
For further information see: www.dkimages.com

Jacket images: *Front*: PunchStock: Stockbyte Platinum

All other images © Dorling Kindersley
For further information see: www.dkimages.com

Thanks to Constance Novis for proofreading, to Hilary Bird for the index, and to Margaret Parrish for Americanization.

Thanks to the following people from the USC Shoah Foundation Institute: Douglas Greenberg, Professor of History and Executive Director, Karen Jungblut, Director, Archival Access & Special Projects, Kim Simon, Director, Partnerships & International Programs

Thanks also to the following people whose testimonies are featured in this book: Alexander Van Kollem, Aniela Ania Radek, Bernard Schuster, Claire Boren, Demetrius Dvoichenko-Markov, Diana Golden, Emma Mogilensky, Eric Richmond, Felicia Carmelly, Fred Baer, Fred Spiegel, Henry Greenblatt, Henry Oster, Jacob Sandbrand, Julia Lentini, Leon Bass, Leonie Hilton, Lola Putt, Mayer Schondorf, Michelle Cohen-Rodriguez, Peter Hersch, Peter Less, Renée Firestone, Rose Silberberg-Skier, Ruth Gruber, Sigi Hart, Thea Rumstein, Vera Eden, Vera Gissing, William Williams

The publisher wishes to acknowledge the following publications. Every effort has been made to contact the rights owners in each case but the publisher would welcome information on any omissions.
p18 *The Promised Land*, by Mary Antin (Penguin Books); p19 Adapted and abridged from *Chasing Shadows*, by Hugo Gryn with Naomi Gryn (Penguin Books) and from the documentary film *The Sabbath Bride*; p38 *The Holocaust, The Jewish Tragedy* by Sir Martin Gilbert (Harper Collins); p49 *Kristallnacht at the Dinslaken Orphanage* by YS Herz (Yad Vashem Studies, XI, 1976); p93 *Commandant of Auschwitz* by Rudolf Hoess (International Auschwitz Committee); p110 *If this is a Man*, by Primo Levi (Random House/Einaudi); p128 *The Diary of a Young Girl: The Definitive Edition*, by Anne Frank (Penguin Books/Random House); p129 *Salvaged Pages: Young Writer Diaries of the Holocaust*, edited by Alexandra Zapruder (Yale University Press). The publisher also wishes to acknowledge Sir Gilbert Martin whose maps were an inspiration during the production of this book.

CREDITS AND ACKNOWLEDGEMENTS